POWER PRAYERS
−⇁ to ⇐−
Bless Your Heart

BARBOUR
PUBLISHING

© 2014 by Barbour Publishing, Inc.

Text compiled from *Power Prayers for Grads*, *Power Prayers for Mothers*, and *Power Prayers for Men*.

ISBN 978-1-64352-766-6

eBook Editions:
Adobe Digital Edition (.epub) 978-1-63058-073-5
Kindle and MobiPocket Edition (.prc) 978-1-63058-074-2

All rights reserved. No part of this publication may be reproduced or transmitted for commercial purposes, except for brief quotations in printed reviews, without written permission of the publisher.

Churches and other noncommercial interests may reproduce portions of this book without the express written permission of Barbour Publishing, provided that the text does not exceed 500 words or 5 percent of the entire book, whichever is less, and that the text is not material quoted from another publisher. When reproducing text from this book, include the following credit line: "From *Power Prayers to Bless Your Heart*, published by Barbour Publishing, Inc. Used by permission."

Scripture quotations marked kjv are taken from the King James Version of the Bible.

Scripture quotations marked nkjv are taken from the New King James Version®. Copyright © 1982 by Thomas Nelson, Inc. Used by permission. All rights reserved.

Scripture quotations marked niv are taken from the HOLY BIBLE, NEW INTERNATIONAL VERSION®. niv®. Copyright © 1973, 1978, 1984, 2011 by Biblica, Inc.™ Used by permission. All rights reserved worldwide.

Scripture quotations marked nlt are taken from the *Holy Bible*. New Living Translation copyright© 1996, 2004, 2015 by Tyndale House Foundation. Used by permission of Tyndale House Publishers, Inc. Carol Stream, Illinois 60188. All rights reserved.

Scripture quotations marked nasb are taken from the New American Standard Bible, © 1960, 1962, 1963, 1968, 1971, 1972, 1973, 1975, 1977, 1995 by The Lockman Foundation. Used by permission.

Scripture quotations marked ncv are taken from the New Century Version of the Bible, copyright © 2005 by Thomas Nelson, Inc. Used by permission. All rights reserved.

Scripture quotations marked msg are from *THE MESSAGE*. Copyright © by Eugene H. Peterson 1993, 1994, 1995, 1996, 2000, 2001, 2002. Used by permission of NavPress Publishing Group.

Published by Barbour Publishing, Inc., 1810 Barbour Drive, Uhrichsville, Ohio 44683, www.barbourbooks.com

Our mission is to inspire the world with the life-changing message of the Bible.

Member of the
Evangelical Christian
Publishers Association

Printed in the United States of America.

Contents

Introduction: The Power of Prayer. 5

Chapter 1: My Bible—
　The Power of God's Words. 9

Chapter 2: My Faith—
　The Power of Knowing God. 19

Chapter 3: My Friends—
　The Power of Lasting Connections. 29

Chapter 4: My Family—
　The Power of Relationship 37

Chapter 5: My Fears—
　The Power of Trusting God 45

Chapter 6: My Money—
　The Power of Financial Wisdom 55

Chapter 7: My Ministry—
　The Power of Being Real 65

Chapter 8: My Education—
　The Power of Knowledge 73

Chapter 9: My Passion—
　The Power of the Heart 83

Chapter 10: My Health—
　The Power to Live a Long Life. 91

Chapter 11: My Church—
　The Power of Shared Faith 99

Chapter 12: My Personal History—
   The Power of Forgiveness 109

Chapter 13: My Habits—
   The Power of a Healthy Lifestyle 119

Chapter 14: My Future—
   The Power of Pursuing God's Plan 129

Chapter 15: My Home—
   The Power of a Warm Welcome 139

Chapter 16: My Nation—
   The Power of Belonging 149

Chapter 17: My Joy—
   The Power of Shared Happiness 159

Chapter 18: My Peace—
   The Power of God's Serenity. 169

Chapter 19: My Job—
   The Power of a Worthy Pursuit. 179

Chapter 20: My Dreams—
   The Power to Surpass Myself 189

Chapter 21: My Fulfillment—
   The Power of Accepting God's Plan 199

Conclusion 208

Introduction

The Power of Prayer

Blessing! A word that is used to describe so many things—new babies, sunny days, unexpected money—and yet encompasses far more than one little word can truly communicate.

According to the dictionary, "blessing" invokes the idea of a special favor, mercy, or benefit. Naturally, we think of blessings as being positive, encouraging, and thrilling. Who would ever say they didn't want to receive God's blessing in their life?

Several years ago, my husband and I began the process of adopting our precious son from Thailand. We completed the paperwork, received our approval, and began waiting. We had been told to expect a twelve- to fifteen-month wait. A year passed, but nothing happened. Nearly thirty months passed before we were finally invited to travel and meet the little boy who had stolen our hearts.

The wait was painful. In truth, it didn't look to us like a blessing. It looked like one delay after another. But as we look back on those thirty months and everything they have produced—new friendships, chances to encourage others, a published book, and a closer walk with God—we realize that waiting was a gift from God, who understood what we needed more than we did.

The book of Exodus tells the story of Moses, who was born at a difficult time in Israel's history. The Israelites were growing in number, and Pharaoh was concerned that he would become unable to control them. In a desperate, tyrannical act, he ordered all Hebrew baby boys to be killed. Can you imagine? Families everywhere experienced the worst imaginable losses at the hands of their own leadership.

A woman named Jochebed took her much-loved son and placed him in a basket in the Nile. No doubt her heart was heavy as she did this, knowing the outcome was out of her control. The Bible details a phenomenal story where the baby was discovered by a member of Egyptian royalty, was adopted into the royal family, and was given the influence and authority to change lives. Moses would do incredible things for God, including meeting God at the burning bush and leading his people out of Egypt at a critical time.

What looked at first to be sadness and difficulty at every angle was really God's blessing in disguise.

"Blessing" is the pile of presents under the Christmas tree and the ten-dollar bill found in last year's coat pocket, but it is also the difficult circumstances that God allows into our lives to make us more like Himself and to point other people to Him.

As you read these pages and think about your own life, consider the many ways your Heavenly

Father wishes to bless your heart—whether by joy or pain.

> *But as for you, you meant evil against me; but God meant it for good, in order to bring it about as it is this day, to save many people alive.*
> GENESIS 50:20 NKJV

CHAPTER 1

My Bible

The Power of God's Words

You can probably name several people who have some kind of power in your life. As a student, you have to obey the rules your teachers enforce. As a licensed driver, you have to follow traffic laws or face the consequences. As an employee, you have to please your boss, who has the power to hire and fire, promote and demote. Like it or not, your parents have the power to make decisions for your life until you turn eighteen. These people hold the power—granting permission for you to do certain things.

You also allow people you admire and respect to speak to you with some authority. You value their opinions and weigh their words as you make life decisions.

The Bible consists of God's words, the ultimate authority and power for your life. It's not just a reference book filled with stories of the past; it contains promises from God for your life. "The word of God is alive and active. Sharper than any double-edged sword, it penetrates even to dividing soul and spirit, joints and marrow; it judges the thoughts and attitudes of the heart" (Hebrews 4:12 NIV).

When an *American Idol* finalist steps on stage, you expect to hear an amazing voice filled with power and talent. Imagine the sound all of heaven heard when God spoke the world into existence. His words created Earth and everything in it. He called light to be and the oceans to divide. He formed every living thing with the sound of His voice (Genesis 1; Hebrews 11:3). His words commanded creation to happen with unimaginable power.

Now think about your Bible. It is full of God's words—scriptures inspired by God (2 Timothy 3:16). God created the world with words—and it is His Word that you can hold in your hand.

As you study your Bible and learn what God has to say about your life, allow your heart to become full of truth and life. You'll come to know God and His answers to the questions you face every day. You learn how to have a personal relationship with God by knowing Him through His Word, speaking to Him when you pray, and then listening to His voice as He speaks to you.

Jesus used scripture after a time of prayer and fasting when He was tempted by the devil: "Then Jesus, being filled with the Holy Spirit, returned from the Jordan and was led by the Spirit into the wilderness, being tempted for forty days by the devil. And in those days He ate nothing, and afterward, when they had ended, He was hungry. And the devil said to Him, 'If You are the Son of God, command this stone to become bread.' But Jesus answered him, saying, 'It is written, "Man shall not live by bread alone, but by every word of God" ' " (Luke 4:1–4 NKJV).

Jesus knew the Bible. He knew His Father's opinion on the situation, and He overcame the devil with the power of the Word and prayer.

As you pray, remember the power His Word has in your life. When you pray according to God's will, you have all of heaven backing you up.

⇁ Devoted to God's Word ↽

Today I choose Your Word, Lord. Your way is just and right. I will take the path You have chosen for me, and I will walk in the direction Your Word tells me to go. Help me to follow You with all my heart. Help me to keep my heart right so I always do what pleases You. Help me to keep Your commandments. Show me biblical truths. I am devoted to Your Word. I take it to heart so I will not sin against You.

⇁ The Way of Truth ↽

Lord, give me understanding so I can know You better. Help me to keep Your commandments and obey Your truth with all my heart. I want to become passionate about Your Word. Turn my heart toward Your desires for my life. In Your truth I find comfort and peace. Turn my eyes away from worthless things and keep my focus on You. Your truth speaks clearly to me every day so I can live my life according to Your will.

> *How I long for your precepts!*
> *In your righteousness preserve my life.*
> PSALM 119:40 NIV

⇁ LIFE FOR YOUR SOUL ↽

Your Word is perfect, Your principles long-standing and proven over many lifetimes. You revive my soul with Your wise and trustworthy commands. Your Word fills my heart with joy. Lord, help me to realize my mistakes, and please forgive my hidden sins. May the words of my mouth and the meditation of my heart be pleasing in Your sight. You steady me in troubled times with the truth of Your Word (Psalm 19:7–11).

⇁ TO UNDERSTAND THE BIBLE ↽

Scripture promises that I can have the mind of Christ so I can know and understand Your words. God, direct my heart and mind as I study and pray. Show me the things I need to comprehend. Make Your wisdom known to me. Help my heart and mind to be fixed on You. Give me great joy in discovering who I am in Christ and the plan You have for my life.

*Study to shew thyself approved unto God,
a workman that needeth not to be ashamed,
rightly dividing the word of truth.*
2 TIMOTHY 2:15 KJV

⇁ According to God's Will ↽

Lord, I want to please You and do Your will all the days of my life. Forgive me when my own desires rise to the surface. I know that You hear my prayers and that Your Word is active and living in me. I stand on the promises I read in the Bible. Set my feet firmly on Your truth. I am rooted, grounded, and determined to live by faith and do what You want me to do. I will speak Your Word boldly and courageously today.

⇁ Power of the Word ↽

God, I believe Your Word is true, but sometimes I have a hard time acting on it and following through with what I know is right. Help me to stand on Your promises. You have put Your power behind Your Word, and I trust You to do what You have promised.

Therefore, we never stop thanking God that when you received his message from us, you didn't think of our words as mere human ideas. You accepted what we said as the very word of God—which, of course, it is. And this word continues to work in you who believe.
1 THESSALONIANS 2:13 NLT

⇾ Water the Word ⇽

As I study the Bible, the seeds of Your Word are planted in my heart. I pray that Your truths deepen in me. Just as a tree grows strong planted by a river filled with good nutrients, I grow stronger each day through the water of Your Word. I will never fail because Your Word lives in me, and Your Word will never fail. When I gave my life to You, Lord, You started a good work in me, and I know that it will continue until You return.

⇾ Guided by Truth ⇽

I trust You, Lord, with all my heart. In everything I do, I acknowledge You and give Your Word first place in my life. I walk in the light of Your Word, stepping where You shine the light of truth, trusting I am in the right place at the right time to live my life according to Your purposes. I refuse to veer to the right or the left but take comfort knowing that You are always guiding me. I listen as Your voice speaks to me, showing me the way to go.

⇾ Integrity of the Word ⇽

Father, I have great respect for Your Word. I give it first place in my life. Your Word is my umpire, settling disputes and answering questions that I face every day. I refuse to compromise. I set my heart upon the foundation of Your Word and will not be moved from it.

> *Keep this Book of the Law always on your lips;*
> *meditate on it day and night, so that you*
> *may be careful to do everything written in it.*
> *Then you will be prosperous and successful.*
> JOSHUA 1:8 NIV

⇁ LIMITLESS POWER OF GOD'S WORD ↽

Thank You, God, for giving me Your Word— Your promise for all eternity. I choose to trust and believe Your Word above all else. I build my faith and hope on You and the power of Your Word. It is alive and working in my life. I know that when I speak Your truths and apply faith, Your Word will accomplish what You sent it to do in my life.

> *But Jesus looked at them and said to them,*
> *"With men this is impossible,*
> *but with God all things are possible."*
> MATTHEW 19:26 NKJV

⇁ THE POWER OF LIVING IN THE WORD ↽

Lord, You gave Your Word to live in my heart. Father, please allow the seed of Your Word to grow mightily in me, filling me with the power and truth of all You created me to be. The Word is a lamp to my feet and a light to my path, showing me the right way to live my life as a reflection of You on the earth.

→ POTENTIAL OF GOD'S WORDS ←

Lord, You have put Your desires in my heart and set me on earth to fulfill Your purpose. You have promised that You will accomplish Your plan for my life. There is no word spoken by You that is ever powerless. Today I choose to believe Your Word. I stand strong, knowing that You will help me achieve my full potential as I hold fast to the truths in the Bible—Your living words for my life.

→ DEMONSTRATE GOD'S WORD ←

Father, as I grow in Your Word, help me to show others the awesome power of Your Word. Let my life be an example of truth for the whole world to see. Help me to live my life before all people, demonstrating the faithfulness of Your promises found in the Bible. Show people through me that You are genuine, real, and true to Your Word.

By faith we understand that the worlds were framed by the word of God, so that the things which are seen were not made of things which are visible.
HEBREWS 11:3 NKJV

⇾ Answers in the Bible ⇽

Lord, when I feel lost and far from You, help me to find comfort in Your Word. Let Your words speak to me as though You were whispering encouragement and direction into my ear. Hold me up with the power of Your Word when I feel defeated. Give me strength when I feel drained by the pressures of my circumstances. Direct my eyes to the scriptures You want me to read for the answers I need today. You know what I need even before I ask.

CHAPTER 2

My Faith

The Power of Knowing God

How many times have you taken a seat in class, plopped down on a couch, or leaned back in a recliner without a second thought as to whether the furniture would hold you? You had no expectation of it letting you hit the ground unless you'd had an experience of falling. Then you might second-guess your faith in that chair, couch, or recliner.

Faith in what we can see is easy for us. We live in a natural world, and we rely on our five senses to tell us what to expect from the things we do each day. We expect the engine in our car to start when we turn the key. We expect our tires to hold air, and we trust that other drivers will obey the traffic lights and road signs.

The natural can fail us, and does. Yet while we see accidents on the road every day because we or others fail to obey the law, we still expect to come and go each day safely.

Our faith in the unseen should be even stronger. Spiritually, we should have an even higher expectation to see fulfilled the promises God has made to us;

and yet we don't always believe we will receive results when we pray.

Jesus said, "I tell you, you can pray for anything, and if you believe that you've received it, it will be yours" (Mark 11:24 NLT). That promise is from Jesus Christ Himself. Yet, day after day we find ourselves doubting because we can't see the fulfillment of our requests.

How many times have you given up on what you've asked God for because you didn't see it in the time frame you expected? God doesn't work on our timetables. Sometimes it takes time, effort, and energy to move circumstances out of the way in order to make a clear path for the things we ask for, much like moving a physical mountain into the sea.

Imagine you were in a park and you threw a Frisbee. You waited for it to come back, but then you became discouraged, disappointed, or distracted, left the park, and went home. Imagine the next day the Frisbee came back, but you were gone.

When you give up waiting for the answer to your prayer request, it's as though you stopped watching for God to throw your Frisbee back. The answer to your prayer is coming back to you, but you're gone. You never waited to receive it.

God does what He does in His own time. You have to be patient and keep believing that He's working behind the scenes to bring answers for your life. He wants to give you the desires of your heart when you pray according to His purposes and plan. Don't quit believing. Keep expecting to receive what you asked for.

⇾ Praise for God's Indescribable Gift ⇽

Thank You for giving the most precious gift, Your very own Son, so I could live each day with You. There are no words to describe the depths of Your sacrifice, but I know You did it for me. You gave Your first and only Son so You could share life with many sons and daughters. I am so thankful Jesus was willing to give His life for mine.

> *For God so loved the world that he gave his one and only Son, that whoever believes in him shall not perish but have eternal life.*
> John 3:16 niv

⇾ Your Gift Accepted ⇽

Jesus, please be the Lord and Savior of my life. I confess my sins to You. Take my life and purge me from all that is ungodly and of this world. Fill me with new life. Make me a new creature, filled with Your Spirit. I willingly give You my life—take it and make it whatever pleases You. Without You, I am nothing, but in You, I can reach my full potential. Help me to live my life so that I am a reflection of You, pointing others to eternal life with You.

⇝ The Fullness of the Holy Spirit ⇜

Thank You, Lord, for Your Holy Spirit. I trust that the Holy Spirit leads and guides me in every area of my life. You sent the Holy Spirit to comfort me and teach me all things. He directs my steps and helps me to make wise life choices. He shows me Your best for my life. I set my heart on the promise of His presence and diligently listen to His leading.

Do not get drunk on wine, which leads to debauchery. Instead, be filled with the Spirit.
Ephesians 5:18 niv

⇝ Knowing God Is There ⇜

God, I know You are there. Even though I can't see You with my eyes, I sense Your presence when I pray. When I feel alone, I remember Your promise to never leave me. Faith allows me to see the unseen, to trust what I cannot touch. I rely on my spiritual senses to get me through to the other side of the challenges in my life—the challenges that tempt me to doubt You and let go of the truth of Your love. Thank You for always making Yourself known to me when I need You.

⇝ Take Up Your Cross ⇜

Jesus, it takes sacrifice to follow You. I have so many dreams for my life, but they are nothing unless they include You. Help me to let go of the things I selfishly desire and that aren't meant to be a part of my life. Your purposes for my life mean success. I give You my life—I completely surrender.

Then he said to the crowd, "If any of you wants to be my follower, you must give up your own way, take up your cross daily, and follow me."
Luke 9:23 nlt

⇁ Finding Faith ↽

Father, the Bible says every person has been given a measure of faith. I already have faith—You instilled it in me when I gave my life to You. Sometimes I don't feel as if I have much faith, especially when I wonder how You could possibly turn my messy life around. But You are always faithful, and I have to remember all You have already brought me through. Help me to grow in faith. Help me to remember that the more I trust You while facing difficulty, the stronger my faith becomes.

⇁ Asking for God's Help ↽

Sometimes I feel You have so much on Your plate that I should work things out on my own. I know I shouldn't feel like I'm bothering You, but my problems seem small compared to what others deal with. Still, I know You want to help me. You are just waiting for me to ask, so I'm asking—please, help. You know what I'm dealing with. Forgive me for not coming to You sooner. I accept Your help today.

> *God is my helper; the Lord is with those who uphold my life.*
> PSALM 54:4 NKJV

→ KNOWING GOD'S MERCY ←

Father, You love me with no strings attached. No matter what I do or don't do, You show me grace that makes me love You more. Everywhere I turn, Your eyes are on me, caring for me with a compassion greater than the love I could ever experience from anyone else. Thank You for Your promise that Your mercy follows me all the days of my life.

> *For the LORD your God is a merciful God; he will not abandon or destroy you or forget the covenant with your ancestors, which he confirmed to them by oath.*
> DEUTERONOMY 4:31 NIV

→ SEEING THE UNSEEN ←

Lord, I am learning so much. I want to see You in the small moments in my life today. I don't want to take anything for granted, so show me the majestic beauty of Your creation. I want to experience You in all I see. Help me to see the unseen. Give me wisdom to read and understand Your Word. Give me discernment so I know the right things I should do. Open the eyes of my spirit so I can see clearly from Your perspective.

⇀ The Power of God's Protection ↽

Fairy tales and fables always have a hero—a rescuer, protector, and conqueror. God, You created me and gave me life. You are the One who saves my life every day. You have given Your angels charge over me to keep me protected. You go before me and fight my battles, sometimes without me ever knowing those battles exist. You are my refuge and my shield. Thank You for always being there.

> *"For the Lord your God is He who goes with you, to fight for you against your enemies, to save you."*
> Deuteronomy 20:4 nkjv

⇀ Increase My Faith ↽

Jesus, You promised if I believe when I pray according to our Father's will, then I can have what I ask. It's so hard to believe sometimes, especially when it seems my prayer is taking a long time to be answered. Forgive me for not trusting You. You have never failed me, and sometimes I forget that. Help me to stand in faith, knowing that I will see the results of my faith. Remind me that answers come in

Your time, not mine. You are the finisher of my faith, so I hold tight to You.

⇁ THE POWER OF GOD'S CLOSENESS ↼

God, I am depending on my own abilities. I don't want to feel far from You, but I do. Yet being close to You is more than a feeling. As I draw closer to You, I know You will draw closer to me. Your presence gives me an inner strength that is not my own. Let me experience You as if You were standing close enough that I could feel Your breath on my face.

What other great nation has gods that are intimate with them the way GOD, our God, is with us, always ready to listen to us?
DEUTERONOMY 4:7 MSG

⇁ EXPERIENCING GOD'S STRENGTH ↼

Life's demands seem heavier than ever before. I am taking a moment right now to recharge my soul with Your strength. Remind me that my help comes from You—whatever I need. You are my power source, and I'm plugging in right now. Fill me up physically, mentally, and emotionally. Thank You that I don't have to go through my life alone. You are always there to recharge me when my power supply is running low. I rest in You today.

*God is my strength and power,
and He makes my way perfect.*
2 SAMUEL 22:33 NKJV

⇁ Praying God's Words ↽

I don't have to worry about my problems today. You are giving me the answers I need to change my life. Hebrews 4:12 says Your Word is alive and active, sharper than a double-edged sword. When I speak and pray the scriptures, I am agreeing with You in what You want to do on the earth and in my life. I attach my faith to Your words, and You give life to the desires of my heart. As I pray today, I know Your power is released to answer my prayers.

CHAPTER 3
My Friends

The Power of Lasting Connections

When you meet someone you feel you've known all your life, it's easy to open up, take off your mask, and let them experience the *real* you. You're comfortable with them, and it's easy to share your life with them. A good friend is one of the greatest treasures you'll find.

God made us to thrive as social beings, and the exchange between friends is essential. Friends offer love, support, and companionship. Because friends give advice and have a strong influence, you must choose them very carefully. A true friend provides wise counsel, encouragement, and unconditional love.

Those friends closest to you encourage you to be yourself at all times. You don't have to be on guard because you know they won't misjudge or hurt you. You can laugh, cry, and safely share the deepest secrets of your soul with a true friend.

Now, friendship isn't easy—it's the rough times that you go through together that connect your souls. It takes courage to share yourself, effort to take risks and commit to each other.

An amazing story of friendship unfolded in 1 and 2 Samuel. David and Jonathan swore their loyalty to each other. "Now when he had finished speaking to Saul, the soul of Jonathan was knit to the soul of David, and Jonathan loved him as his own soul. Saul took him that day, and would not let him go home to his father's house anymore. Then Jonathan and David made a covenant, because he loved him as his own soul" (1 Samuel 18:1–3 NKJV).

They remained loyal to each other, although their friendship was challenged by daunting obstacles. Jonathan's father, King Saul, chased after David to kill him because David had been appointed the next king of Israel by the prophet Samuel. Jonathan risked his father's enmity by helping David.

God has divine connections for your life—people who will help you grow in Christ and support you as together you strive to accomplish the plan God has for you. Every person you meet adds to or subtracts from your life. It's important to fill your time with the right people.

Ask God to direct you in your relationships. Examine them. Are there unhealthy relationships that need to be severed? Ask Him to show you how to do that.

As you apply God's wisdom to your life and spend time with people He's brought into your life, your friendships will become for a season or a lifetime the healthy two-way commitments that mark balanced relationships.

⇀ Thanks for My Friends ↽

Thank You, Lord, for my friends. I appreciate that they accept me for who I am and encourage me to grow in my relationship with You. They want to see me succeed in every area of my life. They are there for me when I need them, concerned for my life just as I am for theirs. Thank You for the courage to be open and truthful with them. You have joined our hearts together with Your love.

*The soul of Jonathan was knit to the soul of David,
and Jonathan loved him as his own soul.*
1 Samuel 18:1 nkjv

⇀ To Be a Better Friend ↽

Father, help me to be sensitive to the people around me. When I am tempted to make things all about me, remind me that You created me for friendship. I want to be a better friend. Help me to prefer others to myself. I want to be a better listener so I really hear my friends. I want to help them if I can in the things that concern them. Let my words encourage them. Show me how to strengthen them with Your goodness.

⇢ Choosing Friends Wisely

Your Word says two are better than one, because if one falls, there will be someone to lift that person up. Lord, I ask for divine connections, good friends only You can give. Help me to let go of relationships that are unhealthy and negative. I want friends who speak and live positively, who inspire and encourage but also tell me the truth when I need to hear it. Give me wisdom today in the relationships I choose.

*The godly give good advice to their friends;
the wicked lead them astray.*
Proverbs 12:26 nlt

⇢ When Friendships Fail ⇠

I'm hurt, angry, and finding it difficult to forgive. I thought my friend and I would be there for each other forever. Help me to handle feelings of rejection. Help me to forgive, and if it's Your will for this person to be in my life, then help us to be reconciled to each other so we can share our lives again. And if not, show me how to move forward without my friend.

⇢ Hurt by a Friend ⇠

Lord, I feel I opened my heart to my friend and it was stomped on. I'm so hurt. Whether my friend did it on purpose or not, the pain is the same. And I'm supposed to forgive? I don't know what to say. I need a little time to distance myself from what happened. Help me to find the words to express my feelings, and please do a work in my heart so I can let go of the pain and forgive.

> *Love prospers when a fault is forgiven,*
> *but dwelling on it separates close friends.*
> Proverbs 17:9 nlt

⇁ A Firmly Founded Friendship ↽

I want to do what it takes to build lasting friendships with people You have put in my life, Lord. My friends are important to me. Yet life is busy, and sometimes I put the things I need to do to get ahead before my relationships. Lord, help me to establish a firm foundation of loyalty, trust, honesty, and integrity in my friendships. When our eyes are on You, we will remain strong in our commitment to You and to one another. Help me to discern when I need to drop a task and be there for my friends.

⇁ Truthful Friendship ↽

The Bible says that as iron sharpens iron, so true friends sharpen the hearts and minds of one another. God, I want to have relationships that are true and honest. Help me to tell the truth in the most gentle and positive way. I want my friends to know the truth about me and about the things that concern them. When they ask my advice, help me to share truth and wisdom from You that will help them grow in their relationship with You. Show them that I love them and want Your best for their lives.

*The godly give good advice to their friends;
the wicked lead them astray.*
PROVERBS 12:26 NLT

⇥ To Look to the Heart ⇤

You know the hearts of everyone, Lord. At first glance, all I see is outward appearance. I want to be a good judge of character. Help me to be discerning. Make me aware when I am being negatively influenced or manipulated. Teach me what I need to know to be a quality friend, and show me the hearts of my friends.

*As for those who were held in high esteem—
whatever they were makes no difference to me;
God does not show favoritism.*
GALATIANS 2:6 NIV

⇥ Pleasing God Instead of People ⇤

Lord, help me to make friends with people who like me for me. Don't let me fall into the trap of trying to win friends by doing things that will entertain or please them. Help me to be a leader and not a follower. The only One I want to please is You. Give me courage when I find myself in the wrong crowd. Help me stay balanced in my friendships, so I will always seek to please You rather than other people.

⇾ In the Face of Prejudice ⇽

All men and women are equal in Your sight. Jesus died for every one of us, no matter where we come from or what color our skin is. Help me not to value one relationship over another because of influence, wealth, intellect, or race. Help me to see others from Your perspective, no matter how different other people are from me. Help me to love them and learn from the differences we have.

> *Therefore, accept each other*
> *just as Christ has accepted you*
> *so that God will be given glory.*
> Romans 15:7 nlt

⇾ To Be There for Others ⇽

Thank You, Lord, for the rich blessings You have given me in my understanding friends. No matter what challenges we face, we face them together. Help me always to be there for them. No matter what they are facing, give me the patience to stand with them, no matter how long it takes. Even when things that concern them don't seem all that important to me, remind me that they would be there for me if I needed them. Help me to remember them in my prayers, and remind me that my relationships with them are centered in our faith in You.

⇾ Pure Motives ⇽

Lord, help me to examine my motives in pursuit of friendship. Why do I seek relationships with certain people? Give me the courage to look truthfully into my heart and see my true intentions. Sometimes I think a relationship with a certain person might help me look better in the eyes of others. I am ambitious, but I know it's wrong to use people to get what I want. You supply everything I need. Help me to maintain right and pure relationships before You.

To flatter friends is to lay a trap for their feet.
PROVERBS 29:5 NLT

CHAPTER 4

My Family

The Power of Relationship

If you look across the sea of people at various events, you quickly realize families can take various shapes. Today we have grandparents raising grandchildren, single moms and dads, and siblings raising younger siblings.

No matter what your family looks like, God purposefully placed you in a family. Family is a God idea. He puts people on the earth through families. "I will bless [Sarah] and will surely give you a son by her. I will bless her so that she will be the mother of nations; kings of peoples will come from her" (Genesis 17:16 NIV).

Whether you've lived at home up until now or you've been on your own for a while, changes in your life and the lives of your family members bring challenge and opportunity to grow together. Daily sharing our lives with one another helps us discover how to live successfully with those we love. A positive family environment offers sharing, laughter, hope, and unconditional love.

Home should be the one place where you feel

safe and protected from the hard things the world throws at you. There are the memories, stories, and laughter you shared with your family. There are the times when you struggled and then hopefully grew closer. Maybe you were there for one another in all the time you spent together, all the challenges you faced and achievements you celebrated.

Or maybe you weren't! Sometimes relationships are strained and families break. Trust is broken. God wants to heal those relationships and restore those wounded hearts. Prayer is the first place to start with your relationship with your family members.

Joseph's ten older brothers sold him into slavery. He was their father's favorite, and in their jealousy and anger, they decided they should kill him. God spared Joseph from their wrath when one of the brothers convinced the rest of them to sell him into slavery instead.

Joseph's story, told in Genesis 37, is an amazing one of provision and forgiveness. God used a boy sold into slavery to save a nation—including Joseph's own father and brothers—from famine and death.

You and your family are important to God. Adam and Eve were created from His desire to have a big family of His own. He wanted to be a Father with a loving relationship with many sons and daughters. When Adam and Eve disobeyed God, sin separated Him from His family for what could have been eternity. He sent Jesus, His only Son, to give everyone the opportunity to be reunited with Him. Through your acceptance of Jesus Christ, you became a child of God and a member of His amazing family for all eternity.

No matter where you go, you are always a part of an eternal family.

⇁ For My Parents ↽

Father, bless my parents. They have raised me the best way they know how. As I've grown up, there have been times when I thought I was smarter than they were or that they just didn't understand me. Forgive me for the things I did that may have hurt them. I was trying to find my place as an adult. Draw us closer together and help us enjoy our friendship.

> *Pay close attention, friend, to what your*
> *father tells you; never forget what you*
> *learned at your mother's knee.*
> Proverbs 1:8 msg

⇁ When I've Hurt My Family ↽

I've made decisions in my life that hurt my family. I didn't mean to hurt them. Please forgive me, and I pray they find it in their hearts to forgive me too. I know they may never understand—please let that be okay. Heal our hurts for the words we've said to one another. Help us to better understand one another. Help them understand that I have to go my own way—even if that means making my own mistakes. Restore our relationship, and open doors so that we can grow together again as a family.

⇾ Unsaved Loved Ones ⇽

It's been difficult serving You when my family members don't know You. I can't seem to make them understand. I don't want to argue or defend my relationship with You anymore. Help me to choose words and actions that let them see You in me. I pray they see the difference You have made in my life and that they'll come to know You too.

> *Whenever we have the opportunity,*
> *we should do good to everyone—*
> *especially to those in the family of faith.*
> Galatians 6:10 nlt

⇾ Facing a Family Crisis ⇽

It is so hard dealing with this family crisis. Lord, teach me how to face these issues in a positive way. I feel so alone. Thank You for being with me. I can't be the one to fix this problem for them, even though I'd like to. You're the only One who can. Bring people across my path who I can talk to about this, people who can support me and lift me up. Help me to focus on what I have to do, and keep me from becoming distracted. I give it all to You right now. I know You won't let any of us down.

⇁ For Peace in My Family ⇽

You have promised the peace that passes understanding. Thank You that Your Spirit lives in and with us. My family is blessed in all we do. I thank You, Lord, that Your peace goes with us. No matter how much chaos is going on around us, we can rest and rely on You. Help us not to get caught up in the moments when it seems the world is spinning out of control. Remind us to fix our minds and hearts on You and live in Your strength today.

⇁ Healing from Abuse ⇽

God, You know our history, where my family and I have come from. Thank You for bringing us into a place of safety. You have begun the healing of our hearts, minds, and emotions. Continue to fill us with Your mercy and love. Cover us with a blanket of assurance that the past is past. Help us to let go of painful memories and start life anew today.

They replied, "Believe in the Lord Jesus,
and you will be saved—you and your household."
ACTS 16:31 NIV

⇾ When a Loved One Dies ⇽

Father, I'm not grieving for the one who died, I'm grieving for myself. I will miss our special times together. My heart hurts, and I can't believe they're gone. Sometimes I look up and think I'm going to see them standing there. Show me how to savor the memories we shared. Help my family and me grow closer to You through this sad time. My hope and expectation is in seeing them again someday when You come and take us all to live with You.

⇾ For Stability in Relationships ⇽

Lord, I ask for You to stabilize my family relationships. Help us to overcome the things that cause us to push one another away. Teach us to be steady and strong for one another. Show us how we can honor one another. Soften our hearts and help us to forgive if we feel we've been wronged.

> *He is like a man building a house, who dug deep and laid the foundation on the rock. And when the flood arose, the stream beat vehemently against that house, and could not shake it, for it was founded on the rock.*
> Luke 6:48 nkjv

⇁ When My Family Frustrates Me ↽

God, I love my family members, but they frustrate me. I want to be there for them, and I want them to be there for me. But they sometimes make choices I don't understand. Instead of confronting them in anger, teach me how to pray for them and speak to them with Your love. Like me, they are still growing in their relationship with You and in their knowledge of Your Word. When conflicts arise, show me how to find solutions that benefit all of us according to Your purpose and Your plan for our family.

⇁ What to Say and Not Say ↽

Father, my family member is hurting, going through a painful situation I don't understand. Help me to be supportive even when I have no understanding of what they're experiencing.

Bearing with one another, and forgiving one another, if anyone has a complaint against another; even as Christ forgave you, so you also must do. But above all these things put on love, which is the bond of perfection. And let the peace of God rule in your hearts, to which also you were called in one body; and be thankful.
Colossians 3:13–15 nkjv

⇁ A Fresh Start ↼

I want a fresh start with my family. We've all made mistakes and disappointed one another in big and small ways. Help us to get past our faults and mistakes. Stop me when I'm tempted to bring up past stories that caused hurt, pain, or embarrassment. Remind us of the good times we all share. Help us to be caring and compassionate with one another. Give me the desire and ability to forgive the past, and help them to forgive me. Give us opportunities to make new memories as we grow in our relationships with You and with one another.

⇁ For All Eternity ↼

Lord, help me to recognize that eternity is now. We are eternal beings, and the things we do today are the beginning of forever. I want to spend eternity with my family members. Remind us that each day is a gift and that our time is precious. Help us not to waste it with idle words and quarreling. Thank You for giving us Your wisdom to make the most of every moment; to build one another up in faith.

> *"As for me and my house,*
> *we will serve the Lord."*
> Joshua 24:15 nasb

CHAPTER 5

My Fears

The Power of Trusting God

Fear disrupts your life, drains your strength, and clouds your judgment.

Perhaps you're struggling with the unknowns of your future or the fear of losing friendships or leaving what's comfortable to pursue your dream. When you focus on your fears, you can become paralyzed, unable to achieve the things God put you on the earth to do.

God, your Creator, did not design you to have a spirit of fear, but a spirit of power, filled with love and complete soundness of mind (2 Timothy 1:7). The word *power* in this verse means the inexhaustible strength that comes from God.

The enemy of your soul—the devil—tries to deceive you into believing God is not all-powerful. John 10:10 (NIV) gives you a clear picture of the devil's job description: "The thief comes only to steal and kill and destroy." Fear, his greatest tool, stands in opposition to your faith. The second half of John 10:10 tells us Jesus' purpose: "I have come that they may have life, and have it to the full."

God, through Jesus' resurrection, made a way for you to turn to Him during times when fear tries to take up residency in your heart. God is there *always*, and He wants you to draw strength and power from Him even in the midst of terrifying situations.

It's the ultimate ongoing battle: *Fear vs. Faith*! We struggle to believe the unseen God, trusting Him despite a lack of tangible assurances that all will work out well. The writer of Hebrews understood this: "Now faith is confidence in what we hope for and assurance about what we do not see" (Hebrews 11:1 niv). We can't *see* God, but we have examples in the Bible of the saints who lived by faith. We also draw insight from our connections with other people to better understand a trusting relationship with God.

Are you hesitant to put your confidence in God's promises because you're afraid you'll be disappointed?

Trust means depending on someone or something, especially in a time of crisis. It takes courage to trust God to fulfill His promises when we can't see Him acting on our behalf. Draw strength by thinking about the times you've trusted God. You may not have gotten the exact results you wanted, but He was always faithful to you. Remember the times you've reached out to Him and found Him there for you, and consider each of them as a step up to the next level of trust. God promises to be with you every step of the way (Deuteronomy 31:6).

Learning to trust is important in your journey to

a successful relationship with God and a successful life. What fears are you battling today? Write them down and give them to God in prayer.

⇁ Trusting God for Acceptance ↽

When people laugh at me, I look to You. When they harass me, help me to be confident. In the midst of it all, remind me to praise You. Help me to be brave when my enemies threaten me. Lord, let Your kindness surround me, and bring me under the protection of those who love me because they love You. Teach me how to live confidently in who You created me to be.

> *"Anyone who believes in
> him will never be put to shame."*
> Romans 10:11 niv

⇁ Trusting God with Changes ↽

Every day I feel the tug of transition. I know change enables me to grow and become who You created me to be. Help me to be willing to step out of my comfort zone to go where You want me to be. I want to remain focused on Your purpose for me, never looking back but pressing forward in my journey with You. Show me how to lean on You when I feel out of place or alone. I know You are always with me.

⇥ Trusting God for Safety ⇤

Father, I follow hard after You. I will not be distracted but choose to be at the right place at the right time, every time. Thank You for keeping me safe today. I am secure because You have made Your angels responsible to protect me at all times. Disasters are far from me because I walk on the path of safety.

In righteousness you will be established: tyranny will be far from you; you will have nothing to fear. Terror will be far removed; it will not come near you.
Isaiah 54:14 niv

⇥ Peace for Today ⇤

Jesus, thank You for the peace that You give me daily. Because You have promised me peace, I refuse to be worried about things I don't have answers for right now. You know what I need to know. Thank You for the Holy Spirit You have given to encourage and guide me. He makes the hidden things known when I need to know them. I rely on Him to teach me all things and remind me of the promises in God's Word. You know what my future holds (John 14:26–29).

⇥ Trusting God for Stability ⇤

God, I've done everything I can to make things right, and now I am doing what I should have done first—

I'm letting go! Do what You will with everything I've held so tightly to. I don't need to be in control. I give it all to You now. Help me to leave it with You and not pick it back up. I'll do only what You ask me to do—nothing more.

> *I will say of the LORD, "He is my refuge and my fortress, my God, in whom I trust."*
> PSALM 91:2 NIV

⇁ Peaceful Sleep ↽

Lord, You have promised me peaceful sleep. I purposefully relax my body. Help me calm my mind and settle my heart. I push my thoughts and concerns for tomorrow out of my head. I put my mind on Your goodness, mercy, and love. I remind myself of the many things I am thankful for. As I sleep, I know You are with me. My body and soul rest safely, knowing that You watch over me all night long. Help me to wake up energized and ready for another day with You.

⇁ Facing the Unexpected ↽

Lord, I'm outside my comfort zone. I am dealing with so many things for the first time. I don't know what to expect. I am afraid of what is about to happen. Comfort me and help me to focus on You. Help me to guard my words and respond with Your love, no matter how fearful I am of the outcome.

> *No need to panic over alarms or surprises, or predictions that doomsday's just around the corner, because GOD will be right there with you; he'll keep you safe and sound.*
> PROVERBS 3:25–26 MSG

❧ Breaking Fear's Grip ☙

God, I admit that sometimes fear grips me. I want to be strong in faith, but sometimes circumstances are just too much. Help me to recognize fear and draw strength from You so I can break fear's grip when it begins to overwhelm me. Forgive me when I try to handle life on my own. I want to depend on You, but sometimes it's hard to let go. Teach me how to trust You, since I know You are more than able to deal with any circumstance I encounter.

❧ Trusting God for My Future ☙

My life is an obstacle course filled with things that try to keep me off balance. But I draw strength from You. When I pray, I know You hear me. You make plans for me to have a successful life and a prosperous future. I cannot fail because You are directing me as I look to You for guidance. Thank You, Lord, that no matter how many times I fall, You always reach down to take my hand and help me up again.

> *If God is for us, who can be against us?*
> ROMANS 8:31 NIV

⇀ The Promise of Eternal Life ↽

Lord, please remind me that death cannot hold me, just as it could not hold You on Your resurrection day. Help me to stay focused on You and what I can do for You and others that will make an eternal difference. I refuse to allow the fear of death to keep me from living in the here and now. Once I've fulfilled the destiny You have for me, then I will spend eternity with You. Help me to imagine my beautiful future with You while I live a life transformed today by Your power.

⇀ Hope for the Battle ↽

Father, I am tired and afraid. My circumstances sometimes seem hopeless, and I just want to quit. Your Word tells me to be strong and courageous. I know life won't always be this difficult. Fill me with Your power, and provide me with a way of escape. Hold me up and don't let me fall. Give me fresh hope for the days ahead.

*"For the Lord your God is the one who goes with you,
to fight for you against your enemies, to save you."*
Deuteronomy 20:4 nasb

⇁ Trusting God for Success ⇀

Sometimes I am too afraid to try because I fear I will fail. But Your Word says the same spirit and power that raised Christ from the dead lives in me. Lord, help me to hear from You regarding the things I am to do. I am listening to Your wisdom, and I know that even when I come up short, I am still a success because I am becoming who You created me to be.

⇁ Shut the Door to Fear ⇀

Heavenly Father, help me to recognize the presence of fear, and give me the courage to resist it by faith. I am Your child; I belong to You. Fear has no place in my life. Just as King David encouraged himself in the Lord, I encourage myself by remembering the great things You have done for me. I choose to keep fear out of my life like a homeowner keeps an intruder from breaking into his home.

*For God has not given us a spirit of fear,
but of power and of love and of a sound mind.*
2 Timothy 1:7 nkjv

⇁ Feeling Alone ↽

Sometimes I feel alone and that nobody understands me. Even in the midst of people, I need Your comfort. Help me to realize You are always with me.

I am convinced that nothing can ever separate us from God's love. Neither death nor life, neither angels nor demons, neither our fears for today nor our worries about tomorrow—not even the powers of hell can separate us from God's love. No power in the sky above or in the earth below—indeed, nothing in all creation will ever be able to separate us from the love of God.
ROMANS 8:38–39 NLT

CHAPTER 6

My Money

The Power of Financial Wisdom

Dustin sat with his graduating class in a long row of chairs facing the stage as a board member opened the graduation ceremony. Dustin's thoughts weren't on what the speaker was saying. He was watching his father and grandfather sitting in the stands behind the platform. They were father and son, but their paths in life had been very different.

His grandfather had enjoyed a long and simple life. Dustin had spent many hours after school and many summers following his grandfather around his small seven-acre farm. He remembered the days he chased the pickup truck up the driveway as his grandfather returned home from his long day as a heavy-equipment operator. Grandpa always made sure he had a snack left in his lunch box for Dustin. After snacks and while Grandma fixed dinner, Dustin and Grandpa made the rounds to milk the cow, feed the chickens, collect the eggs, and check on ripened tomatoes or watermelons from the garden. Grandpa retired at sixty-five and seemed to enjoy life.

Dustin's eyes rested on his father. He had never

spent time at home, constantly climbing the corporate ladder. His wife had left him years ago because she said he loved his job more than he loved her. He had been busy, stressed out, and gruff most of Dustin's childhood. Money was his motivation. After his weekend with Dustin, his father always said "Gotta make a livin'" when he dropped Dustin off at his ex-wife's house. The visits became more infrequent. The more money he made, the more he felt he needed, and that had meant less time for Dustin.

I hope I am wise like Grandpa when it comes to life choices, Dustin thought. *He made money serve him, instead of spending his life serving money.*

The Bible talks about money and financial resources more than any other earthly topic. King Solomon, for example, was one of the wealthiest and wisest kings to ever live. His words in Proverbs provide practical advice even for today.

Solomon's wisdom wasn't something he was born with, but a gift from God. And God has made His wisdom available to you as well. If you want to make wise decisions in your finances and all the other areas of your life, all you have to do is ask. James 1:5 promises, "If any of you lacks wisdom, you should ask God, who gives generously to all without finding fault, and it will be given to you" (NIV).

Look to God as your source—He gives you everything you need. He knows what you need before you ask Him—but He still wants you to ask. Ask Him to help you make wise financial decisions and to keep finances in the right perspective.

⇁ Guidance in My Finances ↽

God, I ask for wisdom and guidance as I manage my finances. Help me to plan ahead and set realistic goals. Teach me the difference between needs and wants—write it plainly upon my heart and mind. And then show me how to spend my time and money appropriately. As I grow in financial resources, direct me in knowing where the income should go.

When his master saw that the Lord was with him and that the Lord gave him success in everything he did, Joseph found favor in his eyes.
Genesis 39:3–4 niv

⇁ Content Whatever the Circumstances ↽

Father, I am learning to be content whatever the circumstances. "I know what it is to be in need, and I know what it is to have plenty. I have learned the secret of being content in any and every situation, whether well fed or hungry, whether living in plenty or in want" (Philippians 4:12 niv). But You said I could call on You and tell You my troubles. So here I am. You know what I want and what I need. I trust that You will meet all my needs according to Your rich mercy and love in Christ Jesus.

⇁ The Power of Credit ↽

Credit is sucking the life out of me. It sounded good to establish credit with a credit card. I just got a little behind at first, and now I'm in way over my head. I am sorry that I purchased more than I could afford. Show me how to pay my creditors quickly. Remind me to consider all options prayerfully before taking on debt.

Owe nothing to anyone—except for your obligation to love one another. If you love your neighbor, you will fulfill the requirements of God's law.
Romans 13:8 NLT

⇁ Open the Windows of Heaven ↽

When things are difficult financially, Lord, help me to remain generous. God, help me never to make decisions motivated by fear and financial insecurity. As I give a tenth of my income to You, You have promised to open up the windows of heaven and pour out a blessing that I can't contain. You are always faithful to provide for me. Let my motives be pure—I don't give to get, but my giving produces a blessing. Remind me that the only way to gain true financial security is by trusting in You.

Every Gift Is from God

Everything I have comes from You. Remind me that I am only a custodian of Your gifts. I want to honor You, Lord, with my wealth. Help me to put You first in everything I do. Never let me be deceived into believing that wealth provides me with happiness.

I know what it is to be in need, and I know what it is to have plenty. I have learned the secret of being content in any and every situation, whether well fed or hungry, whether living in plenty or in want.
PHILIPPIANS 4:12 NIV

Learning to Save Money

It's so hard to watch money sit in the bank. It doesn't seem to be growing fast, but it's important to save for my future. Help me when I'm tempted to buy something impulsively. I want to make good decisions and purchase things that will add value to my life and my relationship with You. Tap me on the shoulder and remind me that I'm not just saving money, but I'm investing in my future. And when it comes time to invest in a major purchase, give me peace in my decision—let me know I'm doing the right thing.

⇾ For Honesty in Money Matters ⇽

Lord, help me to remain honest in everything I do. I want to be known as a person of integrity. Show me how to do what is just and right. I want to be fair to those I work for and work with. I never want to be perceived as someone who takes advantage of others for my own personal gain.

Use only one weight, a true and honest weight, and one measure, a true and honest measure, so that you will live a long time on the land that God, your God, is giving you.
DEUTERONOMY 25:15 MSG

⇾ To Be Debt-Free ⇽

Your Word says just as the rich rule the poor, so the borrower is servant to the lender (Proverbs 22:7). I want to be debt-free. Help me to remember that cash is the best option. Give me patience to save up for the things I want and need. Remind me that more is not always better. Help me to pay my debts as quickly as possible. Provide me with opportunities to make extra money, and then help me to be diligent to put that money toward the debt I owe instead of toward something I want.

⇥ As Unto the Lord ⇤

It's easy to get tired and disgruntled at my job. I have high expectations and can easily let others disappoint me. I don't think they see my potential or appreciate me. Remind me to do my job knowing You are my true boss. You provided me with this job so I could have income. Help me to do my best each day and represent You well. Lord, bless everything I put my hand to, that I may prosper and bring honor to You.

*Never be lazy, but work hard and
serve the Lord enthusiastically.*
ROMANS 12:11 NLT

⇥ The Power of Generosity ⇤

Lord, remind me that everything I have belongs to You—You made a way for me to have it. It wasn't anything I did in my own power that brought me to where I am today. Your love and provision have taken care of me. Help me to recognize what I can give in return. You have blessed me to be a blessing to others. Help me not to hold on to things but to share freely with others as You direct me. Give me wisdom in where You want me to give.

⇥ The Power of Tithing ⇤

God, You have asked me to bring my tithe to You. I honor You in my giving as I set aside a tenth of all You have blessed me with. I am thankful for the many opportunities You have made available to me. I am grateful for the kindness You show me and make available from every person I meet. Thank You for Your promise to open the windows of heaven and pour out a blessing that I cannot contain as I give a portion of what You have given me back to You.

⇾ A Right Perspective of Money ⇽

Lord, help me to look at money as something that serves me as I serve You. I refuse to let the things money can buy be a substitute for my relationship with You. Money will never make me happy or satisfy me. My attention and focus is on You, Lord. Help me never to make a decision based on the pursuit of money, but help my heart forever pursue knowing You.

*A good man leaves an inheritance to his children's
children, and the wealth of the sinner
is stored up for the righteous.*
Proverbs 13:22 nasb

⇾ Financial Crisis ⇽

Father, I need Your help. Give me wisdom and understanding in what I should do in this financial crisis. I don't know where the money will come from to take care of this situation, but You do. Forgive me for the choices I've made that could have caused these circumstances. Help me to listen to You more closely and make better decisions in the future. Show me the best way to deal with all this. Please guide me to do what's right for the good of everyone involved so I can resolve this quickly in a way that pleases You.

⇾ For Creative Ideas ⇽

God, You are the Creator of the universe. You knew every idea before it was thought by anyone. You understood every invention before it was dreamed up. Please give me creative ideas for ways to generate income. Help me to be innovative in developing these ideas, and show me what You would have me do with them.

Careful planning puts you ahead in the long run; hurry and scurry puts you further behind.
Proverbs 21:5 MSG

CHAPTER 7

My Ministry

The Power of Being Real

Reality television seems to catch people in the act of everyday life, showing all the world the truth about those involved in sometimes normal—and not so normal—situations. What if you lived your life similar to a reality show, where the world could look in and see the real you, transparent at all times?

Do you ever find yourself pretending to be someone you're not? How many times have you hidden your emotions and told someone you were okay when your feelings were hurt or you were angry? Maybe there were times when you told people what you thought they wanted to hear instead of being truthful with them.

In the book *Unchristian* by David Kinnaman and Gabe Lyons, a major research project conducted by The Barna Group explains that Christianity has an image problem. The study provides detailed insight into the opinions of sixteen- to twenty-nine-year-olds, demonstrating that Christians have almost completely failed in one of their most important assignments—representing Christ to the world.

Today Christians are perceived as being no different than those outside the Church. Christians deal with the same problems as unbelievers. The divorce rate; indebtedness; and mental, emotional, and physical appearance issues are no different. Looking from the outside in, it doesn't appear that Christians have anything to give the world.

People are looking for answers. They are disappointed to find that even those who believe in a loving God are indifferent toward pointing others to Him with the same mission and vision that Jesus demonstrated. Jesus was unconventional. He opposed the religious, man-made interpretations of the law and looked to the hearts of those who were outcasts, sick, and hurting. He cared about the ones society ignored.

God wants us to set ourselves apart for His service. We are called to be examples to those who do not know Him. We have to get outside the four walls of the church and live in a way that demonstrates to others what God is like. Like Jesus, we must say and do only what the Father tells us to say and do. We must be real—true to the Word of God, following Jesus, and modeling His example. He demonstrated love for the lost, those society had thrown away. He came to testify to the truth that God loves each one of us.

As you move from stage to stage in life, ask God to show you the power of living a transparent life. Let Him help you shake off the facade of what you believe others would want you to be and step into the light of God's truth.

⇁ Genuine Authenticity ↽

Lord, help me to be a true reflection of Your heart in all that I do. Help me to take off the mask when I'm tempted to hide my true self. Remind me that my actions should not be for attention, praise, or position. I want my motives to always be pure. Help me to discern my real intentions when I decide to do something. Keep me honest and remind me that I represent You in the choices I make. In everything I pursue, help me above all to be committed to my relationship with You.

⇁ Real Relationship ↽

God, I want to be real in my relationships. I want others to see You working in my life. Help me to shift my focus from myself to those around me. I don't want my life to be consumed by empty religion and man-made rules. May my words be a reflection of a heart that is full of Your love and Your life.

> *"These people make a big show of saying the right thing, but their heart isn't in it."*
> Matthew 15:8 msg

When Others Oppose Me

Jesus, sometimes I am tempted to believe I am more spiritual and deserving than others. I know You don't condone that attitude. It makes me angry when others make fun of what I believe, and I am ready to defend my beliefs. Help me to consider their feelings and the possibility that they don't understand where I'm coming from. Remind me that being right is less important than being Your servant. Help me to be a positive influence for those You bring into my life.

Legitimate Faith

Lord, I don't want to fake it! I'm tired of saying one thing and doing another. Forgive me for pretending to have it all together. I don't want to be a wishy-washy Christian. Help me to trust You and believe the promises You have given me in Your Word. I believe—help my unbelief.

"So when you give to the needy, do not announce it with trumpets, as the hypocrites do in the synagogues and on the streets, to be honored by others. Truly I tell you, they have received their reward in full."
MATTHEW 6:2 NIV

To Live What I Believe

Lord, forgive me when my choices don't line up with what I say I believe. Help me to nurture Your Word in my heart so I grow to maturity. Teach me Your ways, and give me understanding of Your instructions. Allow the values of my faith to affect every area of my life. Convict me of sin when I am tempted to stray from truth. Help me to stay committed to living what I believe as I grow in faith and in my relationship with You.

To Stay Connected

God, there are so many distractions—so many things I feel I have to do. Help me to stay connected to You throughout my day. I want to share it with You and be used by You to reach others. Speak to my heart, and remind me that You have something for me to do today. Lead me by Your Spirit.

> *Walk by the Spirit, and you will not carry out the desire of the flesh.*
> Galatians 5:16 nasb

Fill Me with Love

God, You are love. Everything You do is because of love, and the motive behind those actions is love. I want to be a catalyst of love in the lives of others too.

Forgive me when I think first of myself. Help me to prefer others. Help my love for others to grow. Give me compassion and opportunities to demonstrate it. Lord, it's not about me; it's about You and those You want to touch through me. Help me learn to let Your love flow through me to others.

⇁ For Boldness in Ministry ⇽

Lord, I don't know where to start in sharing my faith with others. When You give me the opportunity, help me to realize You are opening the door. Help me to recognize Your timing and to follow Your leading. Speak to me and through me. Give me Your words that will touch others' hearts and turn them toward a relationship with You.

I am not ashamed of the gospel, because it is the power of God that brings salvation to everyone who believes: first to the Jew, then to the Gentile.
ROMANS 1:16 NIV

⇁ Sharing My Challenges ⇽

Father, You know all I have gone through in my life, all of my hurts and pains. I know I went through those difficulties for a reason, perhaps to encourage others. Help me to be quick to share with anyone who might benefit from what I have endured.

Help me to share how I learned to trust in You as You brought me through each challenge. Strengthen those people with boldness and courage. Give me the words to encourage them to hold tightly to You during their hardships.

⇾ When Others Are Watching ⇽

It's hard to be an example, Lord. I don't do everything the way I know I should. I want to be strong and diligent to do what is right. Help me hold fast to my convictions. Help me to be honest when I make mistakes. I want to encourage others by following You faithfully. Give me courage and strength to live my life to please You so I can say to them, "Follow me, as I follow Christ."

Be an example to the believers with your words, your actions, your love, your faith, and your pure life.
1 Timothy 4:12 NCV

⇾ For a Soft Heart ⇽

God, there is so much I don't know. Sometimes I think I know a lot, but then I realize how much I have to learn. Forgive me for doing all the talking. Teach me to listen to You first, and teach me how to listen to others. Show me how to discern what they are really saying and wanting. Remind me that people aren't always looking for me to solve their problems. Sometimes they just need someone who will be there for them and listen. Help me to be that person.

⇀ Keeping My Two Cents ↽

Father, You created me with an opinion about everything. I make the mistake of thinking that people value my opinion. Help me to keep my opinions to myself and instead share what You want me to say. Use me, Lord, to speak Your Word and Your wisdom into their lives. Remind me that I am to be about my Father's business. I want to be ready to speak a word at the right time—but only if that Word comes from You.

*Keep your tongue from speaking evil
and your lips from telling lies!*
Psalm 34:13 nlt

⇀ Finding the Real Me ↽

Lord, I want to be everything You created me to be. Give me courage to express myself no matter who is around. Help me not to fear what other people think or say about me, but help me to trust You to protect me from potential hurt. Help me to find the real me—the unique person You created me to be. And show me how to express myself in ways that honor You.

CHAPTER 8

My Education

The Power of Knowledge

No matter how old you are, you will find that your education is not done. You may be surprised to find that being a willing student outside the classroom is just as important as the time you spent cracking the books in school.

Everything God created was made to grow, and that includes your wisdom and understanding of the things of God. As a Christian, you will forever be a student of His. You even have your own personal instructor, the Holy Spirit. "You have received the Holy Spirit, and he lives within you, so you don't need anyone to teach you what is true. For the Spirit teaches you everything you need to know, and what he teaches is true—it is not a lie. So just as he has taught you, remain in fellowship with Christ" (1 John 2:27 NLT).

The Spirit of God is diligently at work doing a makeover within your heart so you become a reflection of His image, but He needs your cooperation. Reading the Bible fills your mind with what God says and thinks. When you make Bible time a priority, it will cause you to grow in your faith quickly. Through His Word, you are constantly discovering who He is and who He created you to be.

Your prayer life is your lifeline to growing in God. As you spend time talking to Him and listening to His voice speak to your heart, you come to know Him.

"Jesus said, 'I tell you the truth, the person who does not enter the sheepfold by the door, but climbs in some other way, is a thief and a robber. The one who enters by the door is the shepherd of the sheep. The one who guards the door opens it for him. And the sheep listen to the voice of the shepherd. He calls his own sheep by name and leads them out. When he brings all his sheep out, he goes ahead of them, and they follow him because they know his voice. But they will never follow a stranger. They will run away from him because they don't know his voice'" (John 10:1–5 NCV).

Just as you know the voices of those who love you—your family, close friends, and others—you come to recognize the voice of God. In the same respect, when a stranger speaks, their voice is unfamiliar to you, just as the stranger's voice was unfamiliar to the sheep. You grow in your relationship with God and learn to respond to His direction as He teaches you the way He wants you to go and what He wants you to do.

The more time you spend with Him, the more aware you are of His presence. As you find out more about Him, you uncover the characteristics within yourself that reflect His likeness. His direction and guidance will help you be successful as you transition to your next step in life.

⇁ To Know You, Lord ⇽

Heavenly Father, I am Your child. I belong to You. I want to know You more. Give me understanding of who You are and what You are like. Teach me the things that are important to You so they can become important to me. Help me to put You first in my life. Give me wisdom to choose time with You and to eliminate distractions that keep me too busy for You.

> *I want you to show love, not offer sacrifices. I want you to know me more than I want burnt offerings.*
> Hosea 6:6 nlt

⇁ To Hear His Voice ⇽

God, I want to hear Your voice. I want to know You are speaking to my heart about Your will for my life. Just as the sheep follow the shepherd's voice and pay no attention to the stranger's words, help me to shut out strange voices so I may hear You clearly. Give me patience to listen—and not talk. What You have to tell me is much more important than what I have to say. Help me to practice Your presence and wait on You. Nothing is more important than time with You.

⇁ To Understand the Bible ↽

The Bible is Your Word for my life. Help me to understand what You are saying to me through it. Give me wisdom and understanding as I allow scripture to feed my spirit and fill me with Your strength. I read Your words so I can grow and learn more about You. Bring the words I read back to mind when I need to apply them to the circumstances I face.

You made me and formed me with your hands. Give me understanding so I can learn your commands.
PSALM 119:73 NCV

⇁ Learn to Talk to Your Boss ↽

Lord, thank You for my job and for giving me the support of my boss. Sometimes it can be intimidating to talk to my supervisor. I hate it when my mouth goes dry and my hands get sweaty. Fill me with Your confidence. Give me words to speak and the courage to say the things that need to be said. I was hired to do a job, and I will do it well because I know You are with me.

*Trust in the Lord with all your heart;
do not depend on your own understanding.*
PROVERBS 3:5 NLT

⇁ ASKING FOR HELP ↽

Lord, You know I hate asking for help, but I need to learn to rely on others. Some things I can't do by myself, and You created me to need other people. Direct me to the ones I should ask for help. Remind me to appreciate their help and not take it for granted. Give me words to express how much their assistance means to me. Help me to be open-minded if the way they want to help is not what I expected.

⇁ TO KNOW THE TRUTH ↽

Lord, thank You for making absolute truth available. You came into the world to testify for truth. It is not relative to what I think or feel. Truth is objective and is based on Your Word, the Bible. Help me to know the truth and see it clearly in my life.

*We know also that the Son of God has come
and has given us understanding, so that we
may know him who is true. And we are in
him who is true by being in his Son Jesus
Christ. He is the true God and eternal life.*
1 JOHN 5:20 NIV

⇁ For Mentors ↽

God, You put people in my life to mentor me. Give me discernment so I know who is a gift from You and who is not. Help me to open up to mentors and receive their counsel. Forgive my pride when I think I know the answers. Let me learn from their mistakes as well as their successes. Help me to be a good student. Teach me to apply Your principles to my life and recognize them as I experience the road You have destined me to travel.

⇁ Seeking the Right Knowledge ↽

God, You know everything. All I want to know is already known by You. Teach me to seek truth in a way that pleases You. I don't want to use what I *think* I know of You or Your Word to look good in front of other people. Help me to keep my motives pure. I never want to seek knowledge that is separate from You. Help me to know You by listening to You and observing what You do. I don't just want to know Your Word; I want to put it into practice. I want to live it out loud every day.

⇁ Discovering Leadership ↽

Heavenly Father, I want to understand how to become a leader. Jesus led by serving others. He gave of Himself freely to show us the way to truth. Teach me what it takes to lead as I begin by following You and the leaders You have placed in my life. Give me a heart to serve and the patience to not take shortcuts in the lessons You want me to learn.

> *It is senseless to pay to educate a fool,
> since he has no heart for learning.*
> PROVERBS 17:16 NLT

⇁ Paying Attention ↽

God, as I am learning and growing in You daily, teach me to be attentive to Your instruction. Do not let me forget what I have learned from You. Remind me of the amazing and miraculous things You have done to bring me to where I am today. Help me to stand firm in my faith, not just knowing what I believe but living it. Keep me alert and cautious about people or things that would distract and hinder me from growing in You.

⇁ A Concentrated Focus ↽

Lord, fatigue is the enemy of my faith. I refuse to grow weary in my walk with You. Help me to make You the center of all my activities. Give me a clear perception of my relationship with You, that I may learn Your ways and understand my place in Your plan. Like a beam of light breaks through the darkness, break through my mental fog, Lord, and teach me how to focus my attention on You.

> *Ezra had devoted himself to the study and observance of the Law of the LORD, and to teaching its decrees and laws in Israel.*
> EZRA 7:10 NIV

⇁ LEARNING IN THE CIRCUMSTANCES ↽

God, teach me how to tune out the voice of my circumstances, the busyness of my life, and the noise surrounding me. My situation hasn't changed, but my attitude has. My hope is in You. Help me to focus on Your promises instead of the circumstances that are shouting at me. I open my heart to listen to Your instruction. Teach me to go to the still waters of Your Spirit and find strength. Peace like a river speaks to me.

⇁ THE POWER OF WISDOM ↽

Father, I am listening to Your instruction. I will hide Your Word in my heart, and I will not forget what You have done for me. I want to experience Your blessings. I will keep Your commandments, not just because You said to, but because I love You. Give me Your wisdom, Lord. Help me to gain understanding.

*They won't go to school to learn about me,
or buy a book called God in Five Easy Lessons.
They'll all get to know me firsthand, the little
and the big, the small and the great.*
HEBREWS 8:11 MSG

CHAPTER 9

My Passion

The Power of the Heart

Undoubtedly you've felt your heart tremble at all that's going on in your life. So many emotions: excitement, enthusiasm, uncertainty, pride. What is the fuel that fires the passion in your heart?

The word *passion* can describe romantic feelings; a drive to excel in sports, business, or a dream; or how someone feels about material items they collect. In the context of Jesus' life, *passion* means to suffer. It is to want something so badly that you're willing to sacrifice anything to have it. God's desire to have a relationship with you was so great that He sacrificed His only Son to have the opportunity to be a part of your life for all eternity.

St. Augustine is accepted by most scholars as the most important figure in the ancient Western church. His prayer, "For you have created us for yourself, O Lord, and our hearts are restless until they rest in thee," demonstrates the passionate cry of the human heart for something bigger than itself.

Unfortunately, people worldwide spend their lives searching for fulfillment from something or someone other than God. In their search, they substitute God's place in their hearts with false passions such as careers, sports, and relationships.

Is getting to know God your passion? Is it so important to you that, just as Jesus did for you, you're willing to make sacrifices to spend time with Him? When you are passionate about His purpose for your life, then you're willing to do whatever it takes to live for Him.

In Romans 15, the apostle Paul is clear—it is his ambition to bring the knowledge of Christ to everyone. Paul's dramatic encounter with Jesus on the road to Damascus changed his life radically. Knowing Jesus and sharing Him with others consumed Paul for the rest of his life.

The Word of God says, "He has also set eternity in the human heart; yet no one can fathom what God has done from beginning to end" (Ecclesiastes 3:11 NIV). Often we think of eternity as a future event—our time in heaven—but eternity is *now*. As soon as you received Jesus as your Savior, you became a part of the eternal family of God. What you do today—what you invest your passion in—is a part of your eternal life.

As you discover your passion for the things of God, your desires for success and a meaningful life come full circle. You learn the true meaning of life.

Start living your forever life now, with a heart passionate toward the things of God.

⇁ Growing in Passion toward God ↢

God, I am growing in faith as I get to know You better. I know You first by what You have done for me. You have saved me from darkness and transformed me. You have given me purpose and meaning. Thank You for reaching down and changing my life. I want to become passionate about the things that are important to You. Teach me what I need to know to complete the destiny You have given me. Time with You is a delight as I get to know and understand Your will for my life.

⇁ Passionate in Prayer ↢

Father, I realize prayer is important for building a strong relationship with You. Jesus prayed constantly and consistently. People in relationships talk to one another. I never want to neglect my relationship with You. Help me to be faithful to You in prayer. I want to be open to hearing Your voice at all times.

A good person produces good things from the treasury of a good heart, and an evil person produces evil things from the treasury of an evil heart. What you say flows from what is in your heart.
Luke 6:45 nlt

⇾ When God Seems Silent ⇽

God, forgive me for the times I walked away, too busy or self-absorbed to stay connected to You. I expect You to be upset with me, and I feel guilty, but Your love for me is unconditional. It's hard to trust when You are silent, but help me to do just that. And forgive me for the times when You were speaking and I wasn't listening. Help me to run *to* You instead of *from* You, so You can restore me to Yourself.

⇾ Developing a Passion for the Bible ⇽

Father, help me to make daily Bible study as much a part of my life as eating. Remind me that the Bible is more than a book, that it contains words revealing Your love for me. Holy Spirit, speak to my heart, and tell me what I need to discover each day. Bring what I've read back to my memory so I can meditate on what Your Word is saying to me personally.

*Draw near to God and He will draw near to you.
Cleanse your hands, you sinners; and purify
your hearts, you double-minded.*
JAMES 4:8 NASB

⇾ Being Passionate about the Right Things ⇽

Forgive me, Lord, when I am tempted to love things that are pretty to look at or make me feel good about myself. I want to stay focused on You. Help me to eliminate anything that competes with knowing You. Remind me when my natural desires are not in line with what You would have me pursue. I want to love what You love and hate what You hate. Help me to get rid of things in my life that keep me from serving You with all that I am.

⇾ What Pleases God ⇽

God, I want to be passionate about the purpose You have for me. Show me the things in my life that please You, and give me the courage and strength to pursue those things. Keep my purpose before me, fill my heart, and give me right motives to accomplish all You have set before me. As long as You are with me and my focus is on what pleases You, I cannot fail.

*How much more shall the blood of Christ,
who through the eternal Spirit offered Himself
without spot to God, cleanse your conscience
from dead works to serve the living God?*
Hebrews 9:14 nkjv

⇾ When I've Been Hurt ⇽

God, teach me to guard my heart above all else, because it determines the course of my life. I want to learn how to keep painful experiences from destroying me. I refuse to replay what happened over and over in my mind. Help me to let go of it. I don't want to think about the people involved, so help me to let them go by forgiving them. I ask You, Holy Spirit, to do a mighty work in my heart right now. Take what the enemy of my soul meant to harm me and turn it for my good.

→ For a Restored Soul ←

Lord, in pursuit of what I thought should be my passion, my soul has been wounded. I am here to ask You for encouragement and strength. I'm not a quitter, but I need to make some major heart adjustments. Guide me with Your Word, and speak to me through preaching and teaching. Show me how to ask for help, and bring people who love me and Your Word into my life to give me godly counsel.

> *He restores my soul; He leads me in the paths*
> *of righteousness for His name's sake.*
> PSALM 23:3 NKJV

→ Standing Up for My Faith ←

Heavenly Father, I want to let my light shine before all people. Teach me to live and act in a way that speaks Your truth to others. Fill me with an undying passion to see lives changed for Your glory. When I'm called to defend my faith, help me to do it in love, with gentleness and respect.

Let the message about Christ, in all its richness, fill your lives. Teach and counsel each other with all the wisdom he gives. Sing psalms and hymns and spiritual songs to God with thankful hearts.
COLOSSIANS 3:16 NLT

⇥ THE PURSUIT OF DILIGENCE ⇤

Lord, in all I do in pursuit of You, help me to be diligent. Help me to stay on task and accomplish my work faithfully and responsibly. No matter what work is set before me, I want to be motivated to do it as though I am doing it for You and not for others.

⇥ WHEN OVERCOME WITH COMPASSION FOR OTHERS ⇤

Lord, I appreciate You giving me sensitivity toward others. It makes me who I am. Yet, honestly, I am worn out from caring for others. There is so much drama in the lives of my friends and family members, and I can't give when I'm exhausted emotionally. Instruct me in Your wisdom as to whom I should give my time. Show me when and where to take time for myself. Help me to know when I need to stop giving to others and take care of myself.

→ Waiting on God ←

My feet are positioned at the starting line. I'm ready to run the race. All I need now is Your signal for me to begin it. I believe I've found my passion, and I'm ready to act on it, but I know I need to wait for Your timing. Help me to be patient. Alert me to what I still need to do in making my preparations.

> *I long, yes, I faint with longing to enter the courts of the Lord. With my whole being, body and soul, I will shout joyfully to the living God.*
> Psalm 84:2 nlt

→ Fuel for My Passion ←

Lord, I am beginning to discover my passion for the things that concern You. I am ready to embrace Your meaning for my life. You know what I need to fuel my passion. Make it come alive in my heart. There is a fire burning in my soul to do what You have called me to do. Set things in motion to help me achieve the dream You gave me. Help me to hold tight to this passion, and never let the fire in my soul burn out.

CHAPTER 10

My Health

The Power to Live a Long Life

God wants you to live a long and healthy life. In Psalm 91:16, He said, "I'll give you a long life, give you a long drink of salvation!" (msg).

There is a powerful connection between your physical body and your emotional, relational, and spiritual health. Everyone has a path to choose: life or death. In Deuteronomy 30:19 (nlt), God said, "Today I have given you the choice between life and death, between blessings and curses. Now I call on heaven and earth to witness the choice you make. Oh, that you would choose life, so that you and your descendants might live!"

When you think of a healthy person, you probably first consider their physical condition, but the truth is that physical health can depend on your spiritual health. In a letter to a friend, the apostle John said, "I pray that you may prosper in all things and be in health, just as your soul prospers" (3 John 2 nkjv). Here John hints that our spiritual health is tied to other facets of our health.

The true picture of health encompasses the whole

person—the real you. You are created in the image of God. Like Him, you are a spirit. That spirit lives in a body, and you also have a soul made up of your mind, will, and emotions. A long life requires balance in every area of your life. You nurture your spirit by feeding it God's Word and spending time in God's presence through prayer and worship. You take care of your body by eating right, exercising, and getting regular health care and the right amount of rest. Your soul requires affirming words and emotional support for strong mental health.

Many people miss God's best when they receive forgiveness for their own sins but hold grudges against those who have hurt them. Unforgiveness holds their soul captive. God clearly commands us to let go and always be willing to forgive. "And do not grieve the Holy Spirit of God, with whom you were sealed for the day of redemption. Get rid of all bitterness, rage and anger, brawling and slander, along with every form of malice. Be kind and compassionate to one another, forgiving each other, just as in Christ God forgave you" (Ephesians 4:30–32 NIV).

The Bible is full of promises for you as a child of God. A specific promise in Ephesians 6:1–3 (NCV) says, "Children, obey your parents as the Lord wants, because this is the right thing to do. The command says, 'Honor your father and mother.' This is the first command that has a promise with it—'Then everything will be well with you, and you will have a long life on the earth.'"

As you spend time with God, be open and willing to receive instruction for living a long and healthy life in Him.

⇾ Promises for Long Life ⇽

God, You have given me so many promises in the Bible. Help me to learn and keep them close to my heart. Thank You for watching over me and promising me a long life. You have given me the opportunity and ability to live according to Your Word. Forgive me when I mess up, and help me to choose life each day. Give me strength to do Your will as I choose right living. As I come to know You better, I pray that I will know with more assurance what You would have me do.

⇾ Choose Life ⇽

Jesus, You offered me life, not just life after death but eternal life that started the day I asked You to live in my heart. Help me to remember that every choice I make is a choice for life or for death, for blessing or cursing. I don't want to live one day less on the earth because of a poor choice I made. Help me to make every decision count.

Today I ask heaven and earth to be witnesses.
I am offering you life or death, blessings or curses.

Now, choose life! Then you and your children may live.
DEUTERONOMY 30:19 NCV

My Path of Life

Father, I know the path I choose for my life is important to You. You have delivered me out of spiritual darkness and into the light. Help me to establish order and live a balanced life. Help me to keep Your ways in all I do. I choose Jesus' example and will follow in His footsteps. Remind me, Lord, that I don't have to travel alone but that Jesus is right here with me. Everywhere I go, as I follow Your instruction, I am in the right place at the right time, and You satisfy me with a long life.

Wisdom for Life

God, I need Your wisdom every day. I know I can't depend on my own common sense. Guide me in everything I do. Help me to be quick to hear Your voice and follow Your direction. When I feel lost, let me be quick to cry out for help. When life gets crazy and I don't know what to do, remind me to call for help and respond to Your wisdom.

She [Wisdom] offers you long life in her right hand, and riches and honor in her left.
PROVERBS 3:16 NLT

⇁ Freedom from Bitterness ↽

Jesus, I'm feeling bitter and angry over the hurt I've endured. These emotions are holding me prisoner. I have to let them go, but it's hard. I want to see justice for what has been done to me, but instead I ask You to heal my wounded heart and help me let go of the pain. By faith, I release those who offended me. Cleanse me and make me new. It's hard to say this, but I'm trusting You. Fill me with Your love for those who hurt me. Let me see them through Your eyes of love.

⇁ Good Judgment ↽

Lord, I am determined to discount my own wisdom and acknowledge You in all I do. Give me a heart that discerns Your ways from my own and those of the world. Help me to be sensible and practical—I don't want to overthink a situation, but I want to respond to Your direction. Help me to see wisdom as the most valuable thing I could attain.

> *If you live wisely, you will live a long time;*
> *wisdom will add years to your life.*
> Proverbs 9:11 ncv

⇁ Living Right ↽

Lord, I realize sin subtracts from my life and right living adds to it. It's a no-brainer, but sometimes my thinking is off balance. Make Your path clear to me. Sometimes trivial things detain me from making right choices. Remind me of Your Word so I make decisions according to Your will. Help me to resist distractions that would keep me from spending time with You. My life is in You, Lord. My hope and expectation for a long life is in You.

To Give Your Life Away

God, I've given my life to You. It no longer belongs to me. I choose to serve You all my life, but I have to remember that or else I fall back into owning my life instead of being a caretaker of it. I ask You to be the master of my destiny.

> *You shall walk in all the way which the LORD your God has commanded you, that you may live and that it may be well with you, and that you may prolong your days in the land which you will possess.*
> DEUTERONOMY 5:33 NASB

A Healthy Soul

God, my thoughts affect my mind, will, and emotions. When I'm spending too much time thinking about negative things, wake me up. Help me to let go of the thoughts that bring me down. Remind me to think of all that is pure and right. I can't change the past, and it doesn't help to worry about the future. Help me to encourage myself by remembering Your promises for my life. Help me to live my very best life and focus on You.

⇁ To Be Disciplined ↽

Lord, help me to be disciplined in every area of my life. A long life requires taking care of myself. Help me to grow spiritually so I can stand firm in my faith. Hold me accountable for spending time with You each day. Teach me what Your Word says about practical things, like what I eat and drink and put into my body. Give me determination to exercise and eat right. Help me to feed my soul with Your goodness. Lead me to positive relationships with people who share my faith.

⇁ Overcoming Discouragement ↽

Father, sometimes my heart is overcome with despair. You know the losses I've faced and the stress I deal with. Forgive me for giving in to hopelessness. Thank You for Your Holy Spirit, who is with me. Strengthen me with Your hope and confidence. Help me to build my faith by walking closely with You and reading Your Word. Show me how to use this difficult time to comfort others. Thank You for saving me from darkness and returning me to the light of Your love.

⇾ God's Way of Living ⇽

Father, help me to always choose what is just and right according to Your truth. Bring Your commands into my thoughts every time I am tempted to go against Your laws. Remind me of my promises to You. When I choose Your ways, I am assured that my life will be completely balanced in the spiritual, physical, emotional, and relational areas of my life.

My child, never forget the things I have taught you. Store my commands in your heart. If you do this, you will live many years, and your life will be satisfying.
Proverbs 3:1–2 nlt

⇾ For Healing ⇽

God, You created me for a long and satisfying life. You knit me together in my mother's womb, and You know every intricate part of my being. You know what I need before I ask, and I'm asking You to return me to good health. You know how my body and mind work, so You know how to heal me. I refuse to let my health be stolen from me. I am determined to fight for it. Direct me to the right doctors, if that's the way I should go. Give me peace to make the right decisions on my journey to recovery.

CHAPTER 11

My Church

The Power of Shared Faith

When you accepted Jesus as your Lord and Savior, you became a part of a large group called Christians and a member of God's eternal family. Jesus told His friend and disciple, Peter, "And I also say to you that you are Peter, and on this rock I will build My church, and the gates of Hades shall not prevail against it" (Matthew 16:18 NKJV).

Church can mean an actual building where people meet to worship God, but Jesus wasn't talking about a place. He was referring to all the people who share a common truth—a belief in His salvation message. The Church is a living, breathing body of believers who share their faith in God and celebrate His love for them. Religion is man-made, with rules that govern a group of people who submit to that organization. But in *relationship*, the heart of man is what God is most concerned about. Church should serve as a home where God's family comes together.

Church is all about the family of God living, learning, and growing together. God the Father enjoys sharing His presence with you corporately and individually. Hebrews 10:25 instructs us: "Let us not neglect our meeting together, as some people do, but encourage one another, especially now that the day of his return is drawing near" (NLT).

There is strength in shared faith. As believers come together, they grow in every area of their lives. You can grow quickly in wisdom and understanding through the exchange of the Word of God and through corporate worship and praise.

An atmosphere charged with faith delivers amazing results. Much as a natural family supports one another and learns to live with and love one another, Christians do the same within the household of faith.

Jesus said, "Again, truly I tell you that if two of you on earth agree about anything they ask for, it will be done for them by my Father in heaven" (Matthew 18:19 NIV). That is some serious power, and when you have a group of people praying and believing God for something specific, miracles happen.

If you don't have a church home, ask God to show you where you should connect with His family. Church is a wonderful opportunity to practice the truth you've found in Christ. You will discover a group of people who love God and will learn to love you. Within your new family, you will find people who will pray and encourage you in the Lord. There are opportunities to serve others in many areas as you grow together.

⇁ Church Family ↽

Lord, I pray for my church family. Give us strength to put aside our differences so we can serve You together. Help us to understand and care about one another just as You care about each one of us. Show me who I can learn from and who should be learning from me. Place me where You want me to be within Your family.

> *You will know how to live in the family of God.*
> *That family is the church of the living God,*
> *the support and foundation of the truth.*
> 1 Timothy 3:15 ncv

⇁ Finding a Church ↽

God, I need a church home. I want to share my faith and learn Your wisdom by spending time with other believers. Guide me to a church where Your truth and love are practiced, not just preached. Help me to be bold and to be first to reach out to people You want me to get to know. Thank You for providing me with friendships that will grow my faith and give me an opportunity to gain and receive support for the challenges I face. Give me discernment so I know where I belong within Your family.

⇾ For My Pastor ⇽

God, thank You for giving me a spiritual leader who loves me and You. Help him to always speak Your truth and never stray from it. Surround him with wise counsel, and give him a heart that listens to counsel that ultimately comes from You. Keep him close to You, filled with Your compassion for the people You have placed in our church. Protect him from criticism. Help him to be watchful over our church family, discerning what is Your best. Bless him and his family in everything they do.

⇾ To Be a Support to Others ⇽

Lord, help me to encourage others every day. Help me to share what I have with others and encourage them. You are my strength, so I will lean on You as others lean on me. Help me to build their faith instead of tearing it down. Help me to be positive and uplifting when people share their troubles with me. When people leave my presence, I want them to feel better than when they came to see me.

Let each of you look out not only for his own interests, but also for the interests of others.
PHILIPPIANS 2:4 NKJV

⇁ To Go beyond the Four Walls ↢

Jesus, I need Your help. We have become comfortable inside our church. Where is the desire to tell others about You? Teach us how to go outside the four walls of our church building. Speak to the hearts of the people within our church family. Share Your vision to reach out to the community through them. Give us the desire to demonstrate Your love to those who are hurting. Grow in us an eagerness to reach and transform lives through the love of God within us.

⇁ More Prayer ↢

Father, You said Your house would be a house of prayer. I ask You to put a burning desire in the hearts of Your people to pray and seek You. Help us to be diligent to pray for You to heal our land, as You promised to do if we prayed. It's great to see people at church, but our purpose is not a social function. We get together to focus on You. Teach us to pray for the things that concern You.

> *"For where two or three gather in my name, there am I with them."*
> MATTHEW 18:20 NIV

⇥ Just Listen ⇤

God, Your family is loud. We talk, talk, talk. I'm guilty too of thinking I have important things to say. Please forgive me. Even in church, so many of us come with an agenda—before, during, and after church. You are the One with all the answers, and we should be paying attention. Teach us to listen to Your voice, to hear You. Teach us to listen when the world is loud and when we find those quiet moments with You. Help us to discipline ourselves to hear You and to be quick to obey.

⇥ When I'm Too Tired ⇤

Church can be demanding, especially when I'm serving You in different ministries. Life is busy, and I'm tired. Forgive me when I want to stay in bed and shut out the world. Remind me that I need the support and encouragement of others, from the spoken Word at the pulpit to the shouts of joy during praise and worship.

And let us not neglect our meeting together, as some people do, but encourage one another, especially now that the day of his return is drawing near.
HEBREWS 10:25 NLT

When I've Been Hurt by the Church

God, Christians should look and act like You, but sometimes they don't. Sometimes I don't.

People shouldn't hurt one another. I want to blame You for their behavior, but I can't. I know they were responsible, not You. It makes me want to quit church, but I know that's not what You want. Help them to see what they have done, and keep them from ever doing that to anyone else. Heal my hurts, and help me to forgive them. Lead me to people who will build me up in my faith, and help me trust the Church again.

For a Group

Lord, bring me to a group of people devoted to You and Your Word. Knit our hearts together stronger than an earthly family's. Show us how to share our faith with one another in a way that propels us to spiritual growth. Let us be an unbreakable strength for one another when facing things that challenge our faith daily. No matter what we face, help us to depend on You and on one another to carry us through.

> *[The early church] devoted themselves to*
> *the apostles' teaching and to fellowship,*
> *to the breaking of bread and to prayer.*
> ACTS 2:42 NIV

⇀ Church Vision ↽

Father, thank You for leaders who know where they are going and where they are taking people. Give us everything we need to accomplish the vision You have given us. Give us the people and the finances to do the work. Show us Your perfect timing for each portion of the plan. Bless every person who is serving, as we work together to accomplish Your goal. Help us to be sensitive to others coming into the church who may not understand what we are doing and why. Help us to share the vision with them.

⇀ Everyone in Their Place ↽

Lord, we are moving forward as Your family. I ask You to bring new people into our church to help us achieve all You want us to do. Give us a burning desire to fulfill the dream You placed in our hearts. Give people wisdom as to where they belong within our church, where the gifts You have given them can best be used.

Speak encouraging words to one another.
Build up hope so you'll all be together in this,
no one left out, no one left behind.
1 Thessalonians 5:11 msg

⇁ For the Lost ↽

Jesus, You came to earth to save all who were lost. Help us to stop expecting them to come to us. Show us the best way to reach the lost with Your love. Help us to live in a way that points people to You. Remind us that relationship is the key to life transformation. Give us discernment about how we are to lead the lost to You. Help us to see them from Your perspective, and remind us that we were once lost too.

⇁ The Power of Church ↽

Thank You for entwining my heart with the hearts of my brothers and sisters in Christ. Teach me to love them, forgive them, know them, and bless them each day. Teach me to pray for them as You lead and guide me in my prayer time. And thank You that I have family I can call on when I need their support and that we can come to You together for whatever we need.

"If two of you agree here on earth concerning anything you ask, my Father in heaven will do it for you."
MATTHEW 18:19 NLT

CHAPTER 12

My Personal History

The Power of Forgiveness

Ah, the past. . .your story of how you arrived at the here and now. When you first meet new people, they often ask who you are and where you come from. Sure, there's no hesitation in telling your accomplishments and what you've achieved to get where you are. Yet you probably aren't as quick to recall the flip side: your embarrassing moments, mistakes, and failures.

Everyone has a past, and no one, no matter how perfect they seem to be, is without fault. We come into the world fallen and sinful because of the actions of the first parents—Adam and Eve.

We start out far from God, but when we find Him, we discover He's made a way for us to begin again. Our lives are transformed through salvation. Our past is erased. We are brand new in Him.

Let's say your life was a book. Everything you ever did or said was recorded in it. And the day you went to Jesus and asked Him to forgive you and make you new, He took that old book filled with your secrets, your sins, and your past and tossed it in a shredder. He didn't stop there. He then took the shredded pieces of your story and dumped them into a sea of forgiveness. The waves carried them far from shore, where they sank to the bottom of the sea and dissolved into nothingness.

Then He turned to you and opened a new book, a new life story with your name on it. The pages are crisp and clean. He offered you a new beginning, a fresh start. Your past is forgotten. In your new book of life, your humiliation, guilt, and regret are gone.

This is what it's like every time you go to Him and confess a sin.

You may have trouble forgetting your mistakes, and you may even have trouble forgiving yourself. But as far as God is concerned, you're brand new. You don't have a history. Your mistakes no longer exist and are no longer written in the book. He doesn't remember your sin.

The devil does. He wants to remind you about it so you keep looking back. When you're focused on what *was*, you can't pay attention to what God's set in front of you.

There's a perception that there are little sins and big sins and that it's harder to be forgiven for a big sin. Yet sin is sin. No matter how big or how small, it separates us from God. It makes us want to run from Him instead of to Him, and the enemy of your soul, the devil, knows that. That's why he wants to make a big deal of your sin.

You have a new story today. Embrace the power of forgiveness. Let go of the pain of the past, and press forward to your new life in Christ Jesus. It's the reason Jesus came to earth—to offer you freedom and peace through your relationship with God. Move forward and don't look back.

⇾ When I'm Feeling Guilty ⇽

Father, You gave me a fresh start when I received Your gift of salvation, but memories of my past sins find their way to the front of my mind. Remind me that You have wiped the slate clean. My past no longer exists for You. Relieve me of this pressure of guilt—my sin is gone! I let go of it today and refuse to let old memories enslave me. I give them all to You. Help me to create new memories of Your goodness and love for me. Thank You for setting me free.

"I will be merciful to their unrighteousness, and their sins and their lawless deeds I will remember no more."
Hebrews 8:12 nkjv

⇾ Moving Past My Mistakes ⇽

God, You don't speak to me according to my past mistakes, and my heavenly rewards are not based on how many times I failed or succeeded. Although I can't erase my past, You can—and have. Thank You for removing my transgressions and filling me with

Your great love and kindness in exchange. Help me to learn from my past and to move forward.

> *"The thief comes only to steal and kill and destroy;
> I have come that they may have life,
> and have it to the full."*
> JOHN 10:10 NIV

⇁ Letting Go of Resentment ↽

Lord, You know my feelings of resentment against certain people. Forgive me for feeling this way. I won't waste any more time or energy on this. I am only hurting myself by holding on to resentment. Help me to let go of the hurt and anger I feel. I don't want to hold grudges. I don't want this to have power over me any longer. I release them to You. You forgave me, and I choose to forgive them. I have no more desire for revenge. Help me to love them with the love You have shared with me.

⇁ Forgive Me for Faking It ↽

Jesus, I've been talking Christianese. I've learned all the right things to say in front of people. They think I'm so spiritual, but I'm lost in the rules of religion. Forgive me for faking it. I desire to have an authentic relationship with You. Consume me with Your presence. I don't care what others think; my relationship is about You and only You!

> *He will again have compassion on us; He will tread our iniquities under foot. Yes, You will cast all their sins into the depths of the sea.*
> MICAH 7:19 NASB

⇁ When I've Judged Others ⇐

Jesus, please forgive me for judging others. I hate it when others judge me, but it's so easy to condemn, categorize, and criticize the choices others make. Forgive me for being close-minded, opinionated, self-righteous, and unloving toward the very people You gave Your life for. They are valuable and precious to You. Teach me to see them that way too. Help me to allow others to express their thoughts and opinions without feeling that my own beliefs are under attack. It is not my place to judge anyone. If possible, let me bring them Your truth in love.

⇁ When I've Compromised ⇐

Lord, thank You for showing me that the greatest danger to my faith can be when I'm tempted to compromise. Truth isn't negotiable, and I want to be on the side of truth. I don't want to compromise the character, nature, or values that come with my life in

Christ. When I do, my old nature leads me instead of Your Spirit. Forgive me and help me to stay the course. Guide me in Your truth so I can stand strong, unwilling to compromise.

> *So now there is no condemnation for those who belong to Christ Jesus.*
> ROMANS 8:1 NLT

⇾ COURAGE TO ASK OTHERS FOR FORGIVENESS ⇽

God, it is hard to go to others and ask them to forgive me. I can think of all kinds of excuses why I don't have to apologize. The truth is, it's so humbling and embarrassing. Help me to swallow my pride. Give me courage to go to them and be authentic and genuine about my feelings. Help me to face their disappointment, anger, and hurt. Give me words that will help heal our hearts and put things right again, if possible. Teach me to be accountable to others with my words and actions.

⇾ A CLEAN HEART ⇽

When people look at my life, I want them to see a heart full of truth. Help me to let go of the hurts hidden deep within my heart. Help me to remove the ugly, hurtful traces of who I used to be instead of who You have helped me become. I want a changed heart. I want to be filled with Your goodness, mercy, and love. I want to become a mirror, reflecting Your image to those around me.

> *Create in me a clean heart, O God, and renew a steadfast spirit within me.*
> PSALM 51:10 NKJV

⇾ FORGIVENESS FOR THE UNFORGIVABLE SIN ⇽

Father, I feel my sin should be unforgivable. I thought it was the answer to my problems, but since then it's been torturing my mind. The Bible says sin is sin—no matter how small or how big. And I know when I ask for forgiveness, You throw my sin into a sea of forgetfulness and never remember it again. I give You this sin today, and I let it go. I refuse to let my past torture me anymore. Thank You for forgiving me and surrounding me with Your love.

⇾ WHEN I FEEL BETRAYED ⇽

Jesus, I know You experienced betrayal when Judas kissed You in the garden. What I am experiencing can't compare, but it brings me comfort knowing that You understand. I am hurt and feel so deceived. How can I open myself up and learn to trust someone again? Help me to heal quickly and forgive without compromising myself.

It is no longer I who live, but Christ lives in me. So I live in this earthly body by trusting in the Son of God, who loved me and gave himself for me.
GALATIANS 2:20 NLT

When I've Blamed God

God, I've experienced a deep hurt, and I didn't know who to blame, so I blamed You. I guess I felt You should have protected me or prevented it from happening. I was just so grieved that I couldn't see the truth. Now I know it wasn't Your fault. Help me to understand what happened. Forgive me for running away from You instead of to You. Thank You for welcoming me into Your open arms even when I was pushing You away. I'm so glad You never gave up on me.

The Benefits of Forgiveness

Heavenly Father, thank You for forgiving me and removing the shame of my sin from me. With all I've done, I am thankful You choose not to hold anything against me. Through Your forgiveness I can enjoy the freedom of Your blessings. And I can forgive myself because You have forgiven me.

Then I heard a loud voice in heaven saying: "The salvation and the power and the kingdom of

our God and the authority of his Christ have now come. The accuser of our brothers and sisters, who accused them day and night before our God, has been thrown down."
REVELATION 12:10 NCV

⇾ THE ULTIMATE GIFT ⇽

Lord, thank You for the greatest gift—forgiveness. I am honored to be a recipient of Your mercy. It's a gift I want to share with others. Help me to learn to forgive others easily. You are my example. When I'm tempted to react to the things that hurt and offend me, remind me of Your willingness to forgive me. Teach me to see things from others' perspective. Give me a heart of compassion so I freely give others the ultimate gift that You have shared with me.

⇾ SECOND CHANCES ⇽

God, You are the God of second chances. Today as I confess my guilt and admit my sins, You are faithful to give me a fresh start. Your mercies are new every morning. Thank You for changing my life by the power of Your heavenly pardon.

Everything that we have—right thinking and right living, a clean slate and a fresh start— comes from God by way of Jesus Christ.
1 CORINTHIANS 1:30 MSG

CHAPTER 13

My Habits

The Power of a Healthy Lifestyle

Everyone has habits—good and bad. Habits are behaviors you do without thinking about them. They are like simple math: they either add to your life or subtract from it. Do you know someone who pushes everything to the last minute? Procrastinating subtracts from their life. It robs them of success at work, in relationships, and in achieving their goals, no matter how small.

What about someone who can't hold on to money? No matter how much money they make, it seems to burn a hole in their pocket, and they never have enough. It goes out as fast as it comes in. That habit of spending subtracts from living a healthy financial life.

Then there are those who are committed to adding to their life. Consider the person who demonstrates healthy discipline by eating right and exercising. We know people who pray and feed their spirits regularly. They are growing in their walk with the Lord, and they exhibit spiritual strength.

The power of living a healthy life is determined

by the positive and negative habits you establish. To achieve your goals, you need to eliminate habits that would take away from your success and to surround yourself with the support that encourages you to add to your life.

The best way to break a bad habit is to replace it with a good one. Let's say before you became a Christ follower you partied every Saturday night. It's hard to sit at home on Saturdays and think about how much fun your old friends are having. Instead, make a commitment to do something else each Saturday night—join a small group from your church for game night or go to a Saturday night worship service.

Breaking a bad habit is simply choosing something different. Stop doing what you've always done, and do something that adds to your life. Become more aware of what you are doing, and exercise control over your thoughts, feelings, and actions.

What habits are taking away from various areas of your life? Do you need to be more diligent with your time? Do you need to be a better friend? Take time right now and commit to establishing a new habit.

Ask God to help you develop an action plan that will help you replace the bad habit with a positive one. You don't have to do it alone. God will walk with you through it. Draw on His strength, and consider asking someone you trust to help you be accountable. Focus on one habit at a time, and work your way to a healthy lifestyle in Christ.

⇁ Addressing Bad Habits ↽

Father, I don't want to talk to You about this habit I have, but I know I need to. It makes me want to hide from You. It keeps me from attaining my full potential, and I want to stop. I know I can stop with Your help. Help me to see the real reason for my habit, and show me how to heal the pain that drives me to keep doing it. Give me the courage to keep trying if I mess up. Help me to stay strong and just say "no" to guilt.

⇁ Forming a Habit of Prayer ↽

I am so thankful that I can talk to You, Lord. Time spent with You in prayer feeds my spirit and fills me with Your power and strength. I am always tempted to come to You with my list of things I want, when I should just sit and listen to what You have to say. Help me to be more diligent with my prayer time.

He [Cornelius] was a thoroughly good man.
He had led everyone in his house to live
worshipfully before God, was always helping
people in need, and had the habit of prayer.
Acts 10:3 msg

⇥ Making Forgiveness a Habit ⇤

God, You always forgive me, but sometimes it's hard to forgive myself. I feel so ashamed when I continue to do things that I've committed to You and myself not to do. The Bible says that once I ask You for forgiveness, You don't remember my sin—but I do. It comes to mind day after day and brings guilt and shame with it. Cleanse my heart and mind of this guilt, Lord. Help me to forgive myself. Help me love myself in spite of my faults—the way You love me.

⇥ Add to Your Faith ⇤

Father, You have given me great and precious promises. With these promises I can live separate from the world, removed from its evil desires. Because You have given me these blessings, I am determined to add to my faith goodness, knowledge, and self-control today. Help me to grow in patience and in service for You. Help me to show kindness and love to others. As I nurture these things in my life, help me to know You more.

*Add these things to your lives: to your faith,
add goodness; and to your goodness, add knowledge.*
2 Peter 1:5 ncv

⇾ Maintaining a Healthy Weight ⇽

Lord, I hate to diet. Instead I want to make a lifestyle change. Give me hope to make a lasting change. I can do nothing on my own—I can only be successful when I rely on Your strength. Show me the right choices that will enable me to change. Teach me how to feed my body what it needs instead of what I want. Free me from emotional eating. Give me a new desire to exercise and live a healthy life. Please send people into my life who will encourage me in this commitment.

⇾ Self-Speak ⇽

God, You know that sometimes I am not nice to myself. I say things that are negative about myself, the way I look and feel. I beat myself up over the choices I make. Teach me to talk to myself as You would. Show me what Your Word says about me. Help me to grow in self-confidence. Show me how to encourage myself in You, like David did. Teach me to talk to myself from Your perspective of who I am.

Words kill, words give life;
they're either poison or fruit—you choose.
PROVERBS 18:21 MSG

⇾ A Habit of Laughter ⇽

Father, I haven't had a good belly laugh in a long time. I don't mean to take life too seriously. Bring times of refreshment into my life. Remind me to look for opportunities to experience the joy of laughter. Point them out to me and then help me to let go and have a good time. Laughter seems to release stress and adjust my attitude. Inject me with funny thoughts when I need to relax and have a good laugh.

⇾ Windows of My Soul ⇽

Lord, one image can affect my thoughts for days. Give me wisdom to protect my heart and mind from the things I should not see. Help me to avoid things that would hurt my heart.

> *"Let's not pretend this is easier than it really is. If you want to live a morally pure life, here's what you have to do: You have to blind your right eye the moment you catch it in a lustful leer. You have to choose to live one-eyed or else be dumped on a moral trash pile."*
> Matthew 5:29 msg

⇾ Devoted to Truth ⇽

Lord, when I am devoted to Your truth, it becomes clear what things do and don't belong in my life. I don't want to believe the lie that truth is relative.

Show me truth in black and white. Help me to break the habits that keep me from living a life pleasing to You. As I am tempted to repeat an old habit, remind me that You are there with me, ready to help me let go. Help me to live according to Your truth.

⇥ Life in Your Word ⇤

God, Your Word breathes life into me. Help me to be committed to Your Word, to study it, and place it in my heart. Bring Your words back to me as I go through my day. Instruct me, encourage me, and fill me with Your words.

My son, pay attention to what I say; turn your ear to my words. Do not let them out of your sight, keep them within your heart; for they are life to those who find them and health to one's whole body.
Proverbs 4:20–22 niv

⇥ Relationship Habits ⇤

Father, I have a bad habit of needing others to pay attention to me. I want them to notice and speak to me. My confidence should come from knowing You and believing I will become who You created me to be. I don't need the approval of others, especially those I don't know. Speak to me when I do this. Help me to stop. Show me how to turn my focus from myself to them. I can't show Your love to others if I'm seeking something from them. Help me to establish good relationship habits.

⇁ A Habit of Selflessness ↽

Lord, I've been self-centered. There are times when I felt like the world revolved around me. Forgive me for such selfishness. I won't die if everything doesn't go my way. Help me not to react so emotionally when something doesn't turn out as I expected. Give me compassion for others and a sense of selflessness to serve them.

Since Jesus went through everything you're going through and more, learn to think like him. Think of your sufferings as a weaning from that old sinful habit of always expecting to get your own way.
1 Peter 4:1 msg

⇁ Stopping Procrastination ↽

Jesus, I've been so bad at putting things off until the last minute. Forgive me! Help me to do the things I should. I want to be ahead instead of behind. Help me to order my day right and to make it a habit to tackle the most obnoxious task first and get it done. When I have the thought, *I'll do it later*, help me to use that thought as a cue that I'm procrastinating.

Then give me strength to act fast and do my task right away.

⇀ The Power to Change ↽

Help me, Lord, to focus on the positive qualities that I have and the Word of God that describes me in the light of Your love. I am an overcomer in Christ Jesus. I am a new creature in Christ, with new thoughts, intents, and purposes. My mind is made new as I spend time with You. Remind me of just how much You love me. I rely on Your strength to help me to make the changes I need to make today.

CHAPTER 14

My Future

The Power of Pursuing God's Plan

Now that you're a graduate, do family and friends look at you as if you should have a plan for the rest of your life? It can be overwhelming when people ask you to present them with the complete blueprint for your future. The truth is, all of us feel lost at times. A comedian once said, "The reason why adults ask children what they want to be when they grow up is because they're looking for suggestions!" Even with the title of recent graduate, it's okay to admit you don't have all the answers.

God created you to succeed. We can get so busy pursuing our future that we can forget that His ways are higher than our ways. Jeremiah 29:11 (NIV) says, " 'For I know the plans I have for you,' declares the LORD, 'plans to prosper you and not to harm you, plans to give you hope and a future.' " We're all guilty of coming up with our own plans, putting them into action, and then hoping and praying that God will bless them.

We all have great plans for our futures. And since God doesn't give us a personal course description laid out word for word for the rest of our lives, we can be tempted to go our own way. *My way or God's way?* It makes sense that the Creator of the universe would have the ultimate plan for our lives; yet, we often struggle for control. Frankly, it's a scary feeling to relinquish total control of our lives to someone we can't see or touch. Faith requires that we live one day at a time following His lead.

At first glance you might think David had it made as a young man. After all, he knew his future—God said he would be the next king of Israel. Although his own family never considered him a candidate, God promised him the throne.

David's story begins in 1 Samuel 16, when he is called in from tending his father's sheep and anointed as the next king of Israel. His future probably didn't play out like he imagined—he didn't go from the sheep pasture immediately to the throne. He had to hold tightly to the promise God had given him. It took many years, and David experienced failures alongside great victories before he ever wore his crown.

No doubt David asked God the same questions you've asked: *When? Why? How? Are You still there? Is this still Your will for my life?* The prayers and cries of David's heart were recorded in many of the psalms as he pursued God's plan for his future. Maybe, like David, you know what you want to do with your life. Perhaps you've had a passion for something since you were a child, but now as a graduate you're finding that God's plan looks different from yours. God is always faithful to lead and guide you. God has set your course, and it's okay if you don't know every single detail of His plan. Take time to pray, and follow His directions one day at a time.

⇀ Waiting on the Future ↽

Just as You promised David that he would be king, You have made promises to me for my life. I know everything You promised will happen, and I'm excited about the future. It's hard to wait on the future I know You have planned for me. Help me to find patience to be content doing what I should be doing now while on my way to achieving the purpose You have for my life.

> *Know also that wisdom is like honey for you:*
> *if you find it, there is a future hope for you,*
> *and your hope will not be cut off.*
> Proverbs 24:14 niv

⇀ Graduation Prayer ↽

God, as I move forward, help me to pursue the future You have for me. I'll find my place and achieve the assignments You give me. All I ask is that You be with me every step of the way, and I know You will. Help me stay on course and use every gift You have given me for Your divine plan. Help me to choose Your ways over my own feelings and opinions. Remind me to run to Your Word and find the answers I need. And never, never let me quit!

⇾ Revealing of God's Plan ⇽

Father, You have placed Your purposes deep within my heart. When I look inside myself now, help me see only what You have planned for me. Give me courage to step out with confidence, knowing that You perfect everything that concerns me.

> *"Eye has not seen, nor ear heard, nor have entered into the heart of man the things which God has prepared for those who love Him." But God has revealed them to us through His Spirit. For the Spirit searches all things, yes, the deep things of God.*
> 1 Corinthians 2:9–10 nkjv

⇾ Finding God's Plan for Marriage ⇽

Lord, I want Your answers for my life. Show me Your purpose and plan for marriage. Prepare me for my future spouse by showing me the issues in my life that I need to correct now so I am ready to love and be loved without emotional baggage or restraints. Heal me from damaged emotions and past hurts so

I don't take those things into my marriage. Bring the person into my life that You chose for me, and make your choice clear to me when Your time is right.

⇁ Giving God Control of My Future ↽

Jesus, You knew that God's will was for You to give Your life so that others may experience God. You gave God total control and submitted to His will. Help me to do the same. I was created for a specific purpose. You have a plan for my life, and I want to complete everything You created me to accomplish. Help me to live my life according to Your ultimate plan.

> *We plan the way we want to live,*
> *but only God makes us able to live it.*
> Proverbs 16:9 msg

⇁ Prayer of Discernment ↽

That same Spirit who raised Christ from the dead lives in me. Thank You that my heart is sensitive to Your purposes and plans for my life. I clearly distinguish between right and wrong; I see the light and walk in it. I trust You, Lord, with all my heart and refuse to rely on my own understanding in any matter. Help me to choose Your way, the right way, every time. I am determined to know You and discern Your voice when You're speaking to me, just as a child knows the voice of a parent.

⇾ God's Plan of Blessing ⇽

The Bible tells me that whatever I put my hand to will prosper. I am blessed in the city and in the field, when I come into my house, and when I go out of it. Your blessing on my life provides for my every need. I ask for Your wisdom, Lord. Teach me to make the right choices and decisions for my life. You make me a blessing because I belong to You.

"I am the Lord your God, who teaches you to profit, who leads you in the way you should go."
Isaiah 48:17 nasb

⇾ Walking toward Your Destiny ⇽

Sometimes my life feels upside down, and I need You to come along and flip it right side up. Point me in the right direction; place me directly on Your path for my life. Please don't let me miss a beat. Help me to be willing always to walk with You toward my destiny. When I become distracted or make a wrong turn, sound the alarm of my heart, and I will run to You. Set my feet back on the right course, and keep me moving in the right direction.

⇁ Moving to a New Location ⇀

Change is hard, and moving to a new place is frightening and exciting at the same time. You know what awaits me at my new location. Give me a good start with everyone I meet. Help me to make an easy transition. Lord, prepare friendships in this new location, people who will inspire and encourage me in my faith. Help me to find a church where I can feel at home with others and with You. I trust You with all my heart and know that You have orchestrated each step as I follow You.

⇁ Looking Forward ⇀

Sometimes I look back at the things that didn't turn out quite right for me. I know I shouldn't focus on wrongs done to me or opportunities missed. You have set a great life before me, and I want to embrace it without the shadow of the past. Help me see the future with joy and expectation. My hope is in *You*!

> *"When the Spirit of truth comes, he will guide you into all truth. He will not speak on his own but will tell you what he has heard. He will tell you about the future."*
> John 16:13 NLT

⇁ Future Success ↢

The Bible encourages me to store my treasures in heaven, and I want to do that, but You have also promised me success here on earth. Today I ask You for wisdom in everything I do. Help me to live my life with honor and integrity so I can bring glory to Your name. Teach me Your ways so I continually walk in Your blessings. Thank You for causing others to respect me because I am a reflection of You. I pray others see something in me that sets me apart and points them to You.

⇁ Planning Ahead ↢

You know my life gets so busy that I seem to get stuck in the moment. Remind me to lift up my head and look to the future. Help me to have realistic and attainable goals. Show me how to balance my life for today while at the same time planning for tomorrow. Remind me to set my eyes on You so I can see where we're going together, with my future on the horizon.

The ants are not a strong people,
but they prepare their food in the summer.
Proverbs 30:25 nasb

⇁ News of Unsettled Future ↢

Lord, the news reports cause so many of us to worry:

economic downturns, threats of terrorism, wars, and natural disasters. You are my rock and my safety. I know as long as I hold tight to You that I have a future. You are my help in times of trouble, and I trust You to keep me steady. Lord, help me to doubt my doubt and to stand strong, knowing that You hold my future in Your hands. I fix my eyes on You and follow Your leading. You perfect everything that concerns me. You hold my future in Your hands.

⇾ The Power of Recognizing Seasons ⇽

Father, I know there is a season for everything. I was born at the right season, and this is my time to live a great life. The Bible tells me there is a time for every purpose under heaven—a time to weep, a time to laugh, a time to mourn, and a time to dance. Help me to recognize the season I am in, and help me to flow with it. I don't want to be resistant. Show me how to bend with Your leading.

> *To everything there is a season,*
> *a time for every purpose under heaven.*
> Ecclesiastes 3:1 nkjv

CHAPTER 15

My Home

The Power of a Warm Welcome

One of the best-known Bible passages on the home is found in Luke 10:38–42. It is the story of Mary and Martha. As the story goes, Martha invited Jesus to be a guest in her home. She took an important first step, but then her priorities became a little mixed up. Luke tells us that when Jesus arrived, Martha got right down to business serving Him. Meanwhile, her sister, Mary, sat quietly listening to Jesus teach. This angered Martha.

"Lord, doesn't it bother You that my sister is just sitting there while I do all the work? Why don't You tell her to get busy and help me?" she complained.

Of course, Jesus didn't view things quite the way Martha did. "Mary knows what she needs to do. I won't take that from her," He said quietly.

The story ends there, but we can learn important lessons from it. Foremost is that Christ needs to be welcome in our homes. He should have membership status rather than just a guest's invitation. He should be part of all we do and all the decisions we make.

We also need to consider how we react to Christ's

presence in our homes. Did you notice Christ never rebuked Martha for cooking and cleaning? Those jobs must be done, but not at the expense of our relationship with Jesus. Part of God's purpose in creating us was so He might have fellowship with us. That's hard to do if we are constantly washing dishes and scrubbing floors. Jesus doesn't mind if the floor goes unswept if it means we will be spending time with Him.

Don't get me wrong—God expects us to be good stewards of our homes. He intends for us to have servants' hearts, but He also expects us to devote time and energy to our relationships. It's not as impossible as it might sound. Pray that God will give you strength to accomplish everything and wisdom to know how to put priorities in the right order. Above all, be sure Christ is honored by the way your home is run.

⇾ Happy Meals ⇽

Lord, You provide what we need to eat, and I am thankful. Our meals might not be fancy, and we often dine on leftovers, but we regularly get servings of laughter as our children share their latest antics. What a special family affair each mealtime is! I'll gladly eat spaghetti rather than lobster if it means we are enjoying one another instead of worrying over how to pay the food bill.

*Better is a dinner of herbs where love is,
than a stalled ox and hatred therewith.*
PROVERBS 15:17 KJV

⇁ A Change in the Guest List ↽

Dear God, do You remember the time we invited a bunch of kids into our home? They all had other things to do, and we were hurt by the myriad excuses. Other people did come though, and we had a good time with them instead. I guess I know a little of how You feel when so many reject You, but You are glad when someone does accept Your invitation.

*For I say unto you, That none of those men which
were bidden shall taste of my supper.*
LUKE 14:24 KJV

⇁ No Prejudice ↽

It seems there is often no room in our hearts or homes for those who are "different." We've established such widely held stereotypes that barriers are hard to overcome. We forget that we don't belong here ourselves; our true home is heaven. You've told us to treat strangers as we would our own children. We'd never reject our own offspring. We must be kind to and care for the strangers among us.

*But the stranger that dwelleth with you shall be unto
you as one born among you, and thou shalt love him as
thyself; for ye were strangers in the land of Egypt:
I am the Lord your God.*
LEVITICUS 19:34 KJV

⇀ Well Reported ↼

I want to have the reputation of devoting myself to every good work, Father, and You've given me clear instructions for how to develop this reputation. I need to raise my children according to Your Word. I need to open my home to those in need and care for other believers. I have ample opportunities to do these things. Make me aware when these situations arise, and show me how to follow through.

*Well reported of for good works; if she have brought
up children, if she have lodged strangers, if she have
washed the saints' feet, if she have relieved the afflicted,
if she have diligently followed every good work.*
1 TIMOTHY 5:10 KJV

⇀ Open to Ministry ↼

Dear God, the childhood memories I have of sharing our home with missionaries and evangelists are clear and happy. I learned so much from these men and women of God. It is my desire to open my home to those who are serving You. I want my own children to experience that blessing and to welcome those in the ministry.

If ye have judged me to be faithful to the Lord, come into my house, and abide there. And she constrained us.
ACTS 16:15 KJV

⇁ Looking beyond the Present ↽

Abigail had a big problem, Lord, and You had a big plan for her. It must not have been easy for her to go against her churlish husband, but she did it anyway. Not only was she hospitable; she was wise. In taking a big risk, she prevented a bigger tragedy, and she was blessed for it. Father, give me the ability to manage my home with kindness and wisdom, as well.

So David received of her hand that which she had brought him, and said unto her, Go up in peace to thine house; see, I have hearkened to thy voice, and have accepted thy person.
1 SAMUEL 25:35 KJV

⇁ At Home with God and Family ↽

I'm so thankful You've given instruction and examples for how we are to live, Lord. Ruth has inspired me for as long as I have known her story. She left her home and chose to help Naomi, but more important, she chose You. How very important that choice is! You must be the center of our home. Please be part of everything we do.

And Ruth said, Intreat me not to leave thee, or to return from following after thee: for whither thou goest, I will go; and where thou lodgest, I will lodge: thy people shall be my people, and thy God my God.
RUTH 1:16 KJV

⇁ Caring for the Lord ↼

Then shall the righteous answer him, saying, Lord, when saw we thee an hungred, and fed thee? or thirsty, and gave thee drink? When saw we thee a stranger, and took thee in? or naked, and clothed thee? Or when saw we thee sick, or in prison, and came unto thee? And the King shall answer and say unto them, Verily I say unto you, Inasmuch as ye have done it unto one of the least of these my brethren, ye have done it unto me.
MATTHEW 25:37–40 KJV

⇁ Given to Hospitality ↼

Showing hospitality is part of Your perfect will, but it isn't always perfectly easy. It's not that I don't want people in my home. It's just that sometimes I fall behind in my domestic duties, and I'd be embarrassed for anyone to come. Please give me the organizational skills I need to care for my family, clean up after them, and still have a home I am willing to share with others.

*Distributing to the necessity
of saints; given to hospitality.*
ROMANS 12:13 KJV

⇾ BUILDING UP MY HOUSE ⇽

So many homes are being torn apart these days, both emotionally and physically. Selfish tempers flare. Hurtful words and drinking glasses are hurled. Faces and walls get punched. It's sad and a bit frightening. You are a wise God. I beg for wisdom to care for my home. Let me uplift my family. I want love and peace to fill our home. Protect us from heated fights and broken glass.

*Every wise woman buildeth her house:
but the foolish plucketh it down with her hands.*
PROVERBS 14:1 KJV

⇾ A PROPHET'S CHAMBER ⇽

Our home belongs to You, Father. You've blessed us with a comfortable place to live, and we thank You. We know You might call us to use our home in an unusual way. Help us to know if and when You are leading us to do this, and give us willing hearts. Surely much joy will follow if we are good stewards of Your gifts. We want to share that joy with others.

Let us make a little chamber, I pray thee, on the wall; and let us set for him there a bed, and a table, and a stool, and a candlestick: and it shall be, when he cometh to us, that he shall turn in thither.
2 KINGS 4:10 KJV

→ TEACHABLE MOMENTS ←

Great Master, I have many responsibilities to You and to my children. My primary task is to lovingly teach and live by the truths found in Your Word. Each command You've given is filled with love and purpose. My children need to know how to trust and please You. I understand that for this to take place, I must constantly be aware of the teachable moments You give me.

And thou shalt teach them diligently unto thy children, and shalt talk of them when thou sittest in thine house, and when thou walkest by the way, and when thou liest down, and when thou risest up.
DEUTERONOMY 6:7 KJV

⇀ Consistency in the Home ↽

God, please forgive me. I know there are times at home when I allow things I should not. I get busy, and I overlook things that should be corrected. I forget that those things learned (or not learned) at home will eventually appear elsewhere and could have a negative effect on many people. Please grant me the strength and patience to teach and discipline my children consistently so that they will always please You.

For I have told him that I will judge his house for ever for the iniquity which he knoweth; because his sons made themselves vile, and he restrained them not.
1 Samuel 3:13 kjv

CHAPTER 16

My Nation

The Power of Belonging

Over the years, Stacey attended many Fourth of July celebrations, and she never grew tired of them. It wasn't until recently, however, that she was moved to tears by the fireworks display. She was sitting in a grassy area with her family surrounded by hundreds of other people. Everyone was oohing and aahing, as is often the case. Children were laughing and adding their comments at each burst of color.

All at once "Taps" began to play over the loudspeaker. The crowd became silent as everyone respectfully stood to their feet. All of the fireworks were red, white, and blue. When "Taps" ended, "Proud to Be an American" began. The crowd remained standing until the song ended. Then the applause was deafening. Many tears were brushed away as people considered the blood that had been shed and the sacrifices that had been made so that they could enjoy so much. With the exception of her own family, Stacey didn't know anyone around her, but at that moment she felt a strong connection with her fellow Americans. They were part of something big—something special.

Stacey felt very proud to be an American. She

thought about the freedoms and opportunities here and the way God truly had blessed her. She was saddened to realize, though, that even Christians have deserted Him.

We've become so proud of our own accomplishments that we have unwittingly shut God out of our lives. As a result, He has become increasingly excluded from our homes, our schools, and our government. We have seen the negative consequences of this in many ways, and at times we've given up hope. But it's not too late. God can still bless this great nation if we let Him (Psalm 33:12).

What we need is for a revival to sweep across our country. It could happen, but it must begin in our own hearts. When God does a work in individual lives, those lives work together, and revival affects their communities and eventually their nation (Zechariah 8:20–23).

Begin today by thanking God for your nation. Seek His forgiveness on behalf of the land. Pray for revival and healing. Pray for your children, and teach them what it means to belong to a wonderful country. Be a part of inviting God back in.

⇁ A Nation under God ↼

Thank You, God, for this great nation. You've blessed us in countless ways. In the beginning, our hearts were turned toward You, but we have strayed far from You. I fear for my children and grandchildren. I want them to experience what it's like to be part of a God-honoring people. Oh, give us revival. Turn us back to You.

Blessed is the nation whose God is the Lord; and the people whom he hath chosen for his own inheritance.
Psalm 33:12 kjv

⇁ A Better Country ↼

I'm thrilled that my kids love their country. As patriotic songs play, they become excited, and they can spot the star-spangled banner a mile away. Just the other day my daughter even included an American flag in her sidewalk chalk drawing. But, Lord, even at their young ages, they are already begging to go to heaven. They are proud little Americans, but they know something better is waiting for them.

But now they desire a better country, that is, an heavenly: wherefore God is not ashamed to be called their God: for he hath prepared for them a city.
Hebrews 11:16 kjv

⇥ All Nations Shall Worship Thee ⇤

*Among the gods there is none like unto thee,
O Lord; neither are there any works like unto thy works.
All nations whom thou hast made shall come and
worship before thee, O Lord; and shall glorify thy name.
For thou art great, and doest wondrous things:
thou art God alone. Teach me thy way, O Lord;
I will walk in thy truth: unite my heart to fear thy
name. I will praise thee, O Lord my God, with all my
heart: and I will glorify thy name for evermore.*
Psalm 86:8–12 kjv

⇥ God Is in Control ⇤

I'm glad You're in charge, God. We hear of many countries that want to destroy us. They can do nothing unless You allow it though. I'm grateful that You are in control and that nothing takes You by surprise. Sometimes I'm tempted to worry—to take my family and run—but no matter where I am, I know that You make no mistakes.

*When he giveth quietness, who then can
make trouble? and when he hideth his face,
who then can behold him? whether it be done
against a nation, or against a man only.*
Job 34:29 kjv

⇝ Exaltation or Reproach ⇜

I have tried to teach my children the importance of living for You. I want them to understand that obedience is good for them and for their country. Lord, if only more people would realize that each individual's righteousness contributes to that of the whole nation. So many of us want Your blessing, but we refuse to live for You. Then we wonder why we face reproach. Forgive us, Father, and make us righteous.

*Righteousness exalteth a nation:
but sin is a reproach to any people.*
PROVERBS 14:34 KJV

⇝ Thank You for Our Leaders ⇜

Managing this nation is not a job I would want—managing my household involves enough challenges! I'm thankful for those who are willing to dedicate their time and effort to govern the people of this land. I don't always agree with them, but I can let them know that. I ask that You would help these men and women make wise choices. Help them also to remember that this nation was founded on biblical principles.

I exhort therefore, that, first of all, supplications, prayers, intercessions, and giving of thanks, be made for all men; for kings, and for all that are in authority;

*that we may lead a quiet and peaceable
life in all godliness and honesty.*
1 Timothy 2:1–2 kjv

⇴ The Lord Will Be Avenged ⇷

As much as I love America, I have to admit it sometimes terrifies me. When I was growing up, I felt reasonably safe. My parents were allowed to raise me according to biblical standards. Although I still have that privilege, the drift toward a humanistic viewpoint is happening at an alarming speed. You won't tolerate this much longer. You will be avenged for the wrong we've committed. Oh God, send revival before it's too late.

*Shall I not visit for these things? saith the Lord: shall
not my soul be avenged on such a nation as this? A
wonderful and horrible thing is committed in the land.*
Jeremiah 5:29–30 kjv

⇴ An Unusual Source ⇷

*Notwithstanding, lest we should offend them, go thou to
the sea, and cast an hook, and take up the fish that first
cometh up; and when thou hast opened his mouth,
thou shalt find a piece of money: that take,
and give unto them for me and thee.*
Matthew 17:27 kjv

It's not that I don't want to do my part to pay taxes. The problem is wondering where the money will come from. My kids think I can just go to the bank or pull cash from my wallet anytime they want something. Sometimes I think the government feels that way too. It's not that simple though. Even so, You got Your tax money from a fish, and I know You can provide for me.

⇁ God-Ordained Power ↽

"What's good for me is good for me; what's good for you is fine for you"—this attitude seems to be a growing trend. It's a "do your own thing" world. No one wants to answer to anyone else. You've given us higher authorities for a reason though. Without parents, teachers, bosses, and government, and especially without You, chaos would reign. We might not always like established rules, but we still need to obey them.

Let every soul be subject unto the higher powers.
For there is no power but of God: the powers
that be are ordained of God.
Romans 13:1 kjv

⇾ The Kingdom Is the Lord's ⇽

I know our government is supposedly "by the people, for the people." That sounds nice, but really it should be "by God, for God," shouldn't it, Lord? That's the only way it can really be for the people. It's like anything else. When You're in first place, everything else will fall into place. I pray more people will understand this truth, so that as a nation we will let You be in control.

For the kingdom is the Lord's:
and he is the governor among the nations.
Psalm 22:28 kjv

⇾ God Gives the Power ⇽

It seems that being entrusted with responsibility brings pride. Even my toddler wants to help put away spoons or forks. So it goes without saying that most individuals who lead a country are glad to be in that position. Father, remind them often that You gave them the responsibility and that they must conduct their duties in a way that pleases You.

By me kings reign, and princes decree justice.
Proverbs 8:15 kjv

⇁ Paying for Crime ⇀

Children are not particularly fond of the discipline that follows wrongdoing. I discipline my children to help them understand that their actions affect other people. As they grow, they must follow the laws of the community and nation, or the consequences will be much greater than what they face now. Lord, please make them good citizens.

And whosoever will not do the law of thy God, and the law of the king, let judgment be executed speedily upon him, whether it be unto death, or to banishment, or to confiscation of goods, or to imprisonment.
Ezra 7:26 kjv

⇁ Elections ⇀

I truly am grateful for the privilege to vote, God, but sometimes it makes me uneasy. With the growing lack of regard for You that has infiltrated our nation, I'm concerned about who will be chosen to lead our country and how the election results will affect the future of my kids. I know You are in control of who is chosen and how they will govern. Although the situation might look bleak, everything is in Your hands. Lord, help me to trust You.

The king's heart is in the hand of the Lord, as the rivers of water: he turneth it whithersoever he will.
Proverbs 21:1 kjv

⇁ God's Choice ↽

As I consider the nations, I wonder how evil people came to be the leaders of certain countries. I have to believe it's because somewhere along the line, people failed to obey You and failed to let You choose their leader. Please help me not to be guilty of disobedience. May I always seek Your guidance when it's time to vote. Please give us strong leaders who will obey You.

Thou shalt in any wise set him king over thee, whom the Lord thy God shall choose.
DEUTERONOMY 17:15 KJV

CHAPTER 17

My Joy

The Power of Shared Happiness

Of all the emotions that can be interpreted as a sign of joy—happiness, pleasure, delight, enjoyment—most have a fleeting nature. Joy stands out as the fullest measure of a person's state of mind. It's the most permanent because it's the deepest. Joy is a measure of maturity. Unlike laughter, joy doesn't well up instantly from a single event. It grows as we learn what is important in life. As we mature, we reject fleeting moments of pleasure based on pride, selfishness, or greed. Instead, we gravitate more toward humility, self-sacrifice, and discipline. We begin to understand the differences between earthly pleasures and a joyful life. As we trust Jesus more, our Christian joy deepens. Joy exists independently of circumstances.

For example, after his successful demonstration of the telegraph, Samuel F. B. Morse was subjected to more than six hundred lawsuits testing his patent. Spending twenty-five years testifying at trials across the country doesn't sound like a joyful experience. But Morse and his wife viewed the court cases as opportunities. They arrived a few weeks early in the city where the trial was scheduled. They visited hospitals and contributed to worthy causes. They helped begin Sunday schools. Neither success nor failure dampened the sunny outlook they shared together. Joy should be shared; a shared joy is a deeper joy. Jesus tells the parables of the lost sheep, lost coin, and lost son in Luke 15:4–32. Each ends with a call for friends and neighbors to rejoice when the lost objects are found. Paul urges the Corinthians to share his joy (2 Corinthians 2:3).

Joy attracts people. Some share happiness with all who will listen—the blessings they have received from others, the triumphs of ordinary events, and their positive assessment even of negative trials. Joyful people brighten a room merely by walking into it.

Of course, a person can lose joy. Periods of sadness can enter the lives of even those who fervently love God. David begins Psalm 22 with one of the bleakest sentences in the Bible: "My God, My God, why have You forsaken Me?" (NKJV). Yet David's joy returned, because the very next psalm begins with one of the most beautiful sentiments in the Bible: "The LORD is my shepherd; I shall not want" (NKJV). When I feel my joy ebbing away, I take comfort in the fact that it will return. Prayer is a powerful tool to bring it back. My brain can't hold positive and negative thoughts at the same time. By pondering positive ones, I drive out destructive ones. Prayers, especially those of thanksgiving, restore to me a joyful outlook.

⇁ Prayer of Thanksgiving and Joy ↼

Give praise to the Lord, proclaim his name; make known among the nations what he has done. Sing to him, sing praise to him; tell of all his wonderful acts. Glory in his holy name; let the hearts of those who seek the Lord rejoice. Look to the Lord and his strength; seek his face always. . . . Splendor and majesty are before him; strength and joy are in his dwelling place.
1 Chronicles 16:8–11, 27 niv

⇁ Contradiction ↼

Lord, I'm amused by oxymorons, phrases of contradictory terms such as "deafening silence" or "jumbo shrimp." The expression "grumpy Christian" should be an oxymoron too. How can I be grumpy when joy is a priceless gift from You? When I start to feel grumpy, let me choose an attitude of joy. If I walk in Your will, You will guide me to what is best for me. I can be a joyful Christian by choosing to put my trust in You.

⇁ Fear and Joy ↼

Lord, fear is ugly and joy is beautiful. When fear is vanquished, joy becomes even more beautiful. So many people have a beautiful smile as they decide to follow You. They have replaced fear with the knowledge that they are following the One who sets aside all fear. I pray I will extinguish fear by remembering that I can put my trust in You.

⇁ Joyful Journey ↽

Father, I pray I will remember my blessings, not my trials. I want to enjoy happiness and not wallow in distress. Help me understand that happiness isn't increased by material wealth or destroyed by unexpected misfortune. Instead, it grows as I center my heart on Your blessings. Lord, remind me that happiness isn't a destination but the way I make my journey. May my joy flow naturally from knowing that You care about me.

⇁ Better World ↽

Lord, at the fast-food place, I noticed a young worker cleaning the area. She was working quickly and happily. She surveyed her work and nodded as if pleased with the result. She understood that she was making her tiny corner of the world a better place. Lord, I pray I'll always have the humility to understand that my worth is based not on pay or position but on whether I make the way better, brighter, or easier for others.

⇥ Full Measure of Joy ⇤

"I am coming to you now, but I say these things while I am still in the world, so that they may have the full measure of my joy within them. I have given them your word and the world has hated them, for they are not of the world any more than I am of the world. My prayer is not that you take them out of the world but that you protect them from the evil one."
John 17:13–15 NIV

⇥ Erasing the Gloom ⇤

Lord, help me make joy an integral part of my personality. May I be filled with joy even when I'm in distress for physical or emotional reasons. May I avoid dwelling on the negative aspects of my life that I encounter each day. Instead, help me erase the gloom and replace it with the warm comfort of Your love. Let me turn to You, the source of my joy.

⇥ Fond Memories ⇤

Lord, I have many fond memories. I'm thankful the painful events of the past have faded. Joyful ones continue to linger. Even when I do remember individuals who were hurtful to me, those recollections no longer have a hard edge. I can forgive and even forget dreadful incidents after the passage of time. Lord, I realize it would have been better to forgive more quickly. Teach me to put hostility behind me promptly. Let me move on to more important aspects of my life.

⇀ Joyful Viewpoint ↽

Father, as evening approached, the landscape had become bleak and desolate. We'd driven through a valley that was deep in shadow. But we topped the ridge and stopped at a lookout. The setting sun gave us a view of gold-tinged beauty. The point of view made all the difference. When I'm in sorrow, I can see joy, provided I allow You to illuminate my life. Lord, keep me walking in the joy of Your light.

⇀ Sharing Joy ↽

Lord Jesus, some days I feel joy so strongly that I need to share it with others. On those occasions, I realize something of how You must feel, because You have an abundance of joy to share with Your people. All we have to do is open ourselves to receive it. May I accept that mutual joy and find ways to share it freely with family, friends, and even strangers I meet on the street.

⇁ Joy without Bounds ↽

Lord, I can easily love my spouse, children, and family. I can be friendly to my neighbors and coworkers. I can wish the best for strangers I pass on the street. But loving those who appear hostile to me is a difficult task. But once I pray for people, I become invested in their success. Their being blessed becomes a reason for me to rejoice. Lord, make joy my goal, not only for myself but for others as well.

⇁ Jesus' Prayer of Joy ↽

At that time Jesus, full of joy through the Holy Spirit, said, "I praise you, Father, Lord of heaven and earth, because you have hidden these things from the wise and learned, and revealed them to little children. Yes, Father, for this is what you were pleased to do."... Then he turned to his disciples and said privately, "Blessed are the eyes that see what you see."
Luke 10:21, 23 niv

⇁ Everlasting Joy ↽

Lord, You have given me many reasons to be happy and even greater reasons to be joyful. Each day, I can laugh for a few minutes and smile for a few hours, but I can be joyful all day. Joy is a deep, long-lasting emotion I can be filled with regardless of the circumstances. Thank You, Lord, for making it easy for me to be a joyful Christian.

⇁ Joy for Today ↽

Jesus, You have said not to worry about tomorrow because each day has enough trouble of its own. I do face burdens and cares. Help me ignore unreasonable fears that make me anxious about the future. Instead, renew in me the joys You have for me today. You are a loving Savior ready to hear my requests and be present when I'm in need.

⇁ Reviewing Blessings ↽

Lord, my greatest happiness comes when I'm fully centered in Your will. Then I see all of the good things in my life. In moments of quiet meditation, I review the blessings that are mine: I live in my home with a loving family; I enjoy the warm fellowship of other Christians; and I work at a challenging job. You have been good to me. Remind me to reflect often on my happiness and exhibit the infectious joy of a true Christian.

⇁ Seasonal Joy ↽

Lord, although I must rake leaves, I can also enjoy fall colors. Although I must shovel snow, I can also watch happy children build a snowman. Although I must race to my car through a spring downpour, I can also enjoy colorful spring flowers. Although I swelter in summer heat, I can also enjoy the longer days outside with my children. Lord, help me experience joy throughout the year.

CHAPTER 18

My Peace

The Power of God's Serenity

Among nations, peace means the absence of war. Within a nation, peace is the presence of law and order. Peace among individuals is the lack of quarrels and disputes. Within an individual, it is inner contentment and serenity. Of all the types of peace, the one we can influence the most is our inner peace. It can be achieved because it comes from Jesus. He said, "Peace I leave with you; my peace I give you. I do not give to you as the world gives. Do not let your hearts be troubled and do not be afraid" (John 14:27 NIV).

When we don't have peace, it's because we look for it in the wrong places. Rather than following Jesus' guidance for serenity, we look to the world. Our secular society, mass media, and competitive culture aggravate the quest for inner peace. Each day, news media effectively increase levels of stress by presenting the latest news in the most verbally and visually confrontational ways possible. Talk shows invite experts to discuss what is wrong with us and what we must do to improve. Commercials insist that we can be truly happy only by possessing certain products.

Listening to these sources leaves us feeling that we are not doing all we can to have abundant lives.

Life is always in motion. New problems, frustrations, and temptations arise. The small annoyances of daily life cause us to lose sight of the fact that personal serenity is possible. We are so thoroughly immersed in an uproar, we scarcely can comprehend anything different. But the desire for peace is never completely extinguished.

We can't control what goes on around us. But we can have better control over what goes on within us. The opposite of peace is stress and agitation. Whatever reduces those negative aspects will allow the positive ones to rebound. With quiet time for daily prayer, Bible reading, and reflection on godly principles, we can anchor ourselves in something more substantial than what the world provides.

I seek solitude in a place that gives my soul room to soar. In a quiet and solemn atmosphere, prayer touches my heart more deeply and I communicate with God more exactly. I think back and see what a full and interesting life the Lord has provided. I've enjoyed a warm home life. I've been given challenges within my ability to bear. God has been good to me. Prayer cultivates a condition of calm and peace. True peace is possible only through God the Father and His Son. The Bible says, "Do not be anxious about anything, but in every situation, by prayer and petition, with thanksgiving, present your requests to

God. And the peace of God, which transcends all understanding, will guard your hearts and your minds in Christ Jesus" (Philippians 4:6–7 NIV).

⇀ Paul's Request for Prayer ↽

I urge you, brothers and sisters, by our Lord Jesus Christ and by the love of the Spirit, to join me in my struggle by praying to God for me. Pray that I may be kept safe from the unbelievers in Judea and that the contribution I take to Jerusalem may be favorably received by the Lord's people there, so that I may come to you with joy, by God's will, and in your company be refreshed. The God of peace be with you all. Amen.
Romans 15:30–33 NIV

⇀ Bridge of Peace ↽

Dear Father, I recognize impatience as one of my faults. When faced with problems, I charge ahead with my ill-considered solutions and ignore the advice of friends who counsel patience. Sometimes I rashly act outside Your will because I'm too impatient to accept Your timetable for solving my problems. I ask You to replace my impatience with inner peace. Please build a bridge that connects me to the peace You provide.

⇾ Rash Actions ⇽

Blessed Jesus, I have daydreams of ways that I might be happier and gain greater peace. Thankfully, I realize that I don't have the wisdom to direct my own steps to peace. When disenchantment sweeps over me, keep me from making impulsive changes that lead to even more turmoil. Instead, help me put myself in Your hands and experience peace in knowing You as my Savior.

⇾ David's Song of Comfort ⇽

The Lord is my shepherd, I lack nothing. He makes me lie down in green pastures, he leads me beside quiet waters, he refreshes my soul. He guides me along the right paths for his name's sake. Even though I walk through the darkest valley, I will fear no evil, for you are with me; your rod and your staff, they comfort me.
Psalm 23:1–4 niv

⇾ Don't Panic ⇽

Lord, David walked through the dark valley, but he saw beyond it to the peaceful waters. When pain threatens to overwhelm my body, when financial upheavals unbalance my mind, when pressures of life descend like menacing thunderstorms, guide me to face anxiety with faith rather than fear. You have offered to carry my burdens, so I will release them to

You. I will pray and take courage. You will strengthen me to handle adversity.

⇾ Hope and Confidence ⇽

Heavenly Father, I have accepted Your Son. He has given me the freedom to begin a new life. I have the peace of a clear conscience, not because I'm flawless but because I'm forgiven. Now I can look forward to a new life full of hope and confidence. I can approach You in prayer as Your child. Thank You that when I bring my wants and needs to You, You hear me and answer my concerns.

⇾ Strange Land ⇽

Lord, like Moses, I sometimes think of myself as a stranger in a strange land. I look around at my community and feel disconnected from it. I realize this world is not my home. I shouldn't grow too comfortable in it. Keep me from becoming entangled in worldly affairs that serve no useful purpose. Instead, unite me with You in peace and harmony.

⇾ Crowned with Glory ⇽

When I consider your heavens, the work of your fingers, the moon and the stars, which you have set in place, what is mankind that you are mindful of them, human

*beings that you care for them? You have made them a
little lower than the angels and crowned them with
glory and honor. You made them rulers over the works
of your hands; you put everything under their feet.*
PSALM 8:3–6 NIV

⇾ Fortress of Peace ⇽

Lord, my prayer is not only that I might hear You but that I might believe what I hear. When I accept the Holy Bible and everything it presents, all traces of worry, fear, and mistrust are driven from me. Believing Your promises builds a fortress of peace. I may undergo trials and experience sorrows, but You will never let the world overwhelm me. As I know You better, I come to experience perfect peace.

⇾ Merely Pleasant ⇽

Lord, when my family and I began our vacation, I asked about their expectations for the trip. The children wanted excitement and adventure. I hoped for something new, different, and invigorating. My spouse had looked forward to a pleasant experience. Lord, sometimes I need to recognize that pleasant and peaceful are worthy goals too. I ask You to open my eyes and heart to accept the everyday joy that is in my life.

⇾ Wonderfully Made ⇽

*You know when I sit and when I rise; you perceive my
thoughts from afar. You discern my going out and my
lying down; you are familiar with all my ways. . . .
For you created my inmost being; you knit me together
in my mother's womb. I praise you because I am
fearfully and wonderfully made; your works are
wonderful, I know that full well.*
Psalm 139:2–3, 13–14 niv

⇾ Sensible Decisions ⇽

Lord, why do I worry about problems that either have minor impact or are unlikely to occur? When I review those problems I worried about earlier this year, I'm relieved at how quickly they evaporated. They all proved to be fleeting distractions. Each day I face the prospect of making decisions and taking actions that might produce unintended consequences. Rather than getting caught up in the inaction of passive resignation, may I focus on making sensible decisions.

⇾ Harmony ⇽

Lord, three years ago I followed an Internet users' group that was vibrant and alive with discussions. Members exchanged hundreds of messages. I came back last month and discovered only a handful of exchanges. I traced the decline and found a disturbing trend. Opinions hardened, and as emails became more strident, voices of moderation fell away. Only argumentative individuals who insulted one another remained. Lord, I pray that my association with Christians never falls into this distressing pattern. May the voice of harmony triumph over discord.

⇾ Prayer of Praise ⇽

*"The Lord lives! Praise be to my Rock!
Exalted be my God, the Rock, my Savior!
He is the God who avenges me, who puts the nations under me, who sets me free from my enemies. You exalted me above my foes; from a violent man you rescued me. Therefore I will praise you, Lord, among the nations; I will sing the praises of your name. He gives his king great victories; he shows unfailing kindness to his anointed, to David and his descendants forever."*
2 Samuel 22:47–51 niv

⇾ Deep Current ⇽

Lord, I saw an unusual sight yesterday at the river. A leaf and a small log floated in the water. The leaf was blown by a gusty wind every which way across the surface of the water. But the log stayed its course with the flow of the river current. Lord,

I pray I won't be blown about by the capricious and uncertain motives of a secular world but that I will be carried deep in the current of Your living Word.

⇀ Sleep ↽

Lord, as I go to bed, my head is buzzing with a thousand unfinished tasks. My mind is thrashing through a hundred ongoing obligations. My fingers twitch at the thought of all the checks I must write to pay bills. Lord, I pray for a full night of peaceful sleep. Give me a deep, restful sleep, with the cares of the daylight hours wiped from my mind. Lord, I settle down in Your arms. I think only of Your calm assurance.

Now I sleep....

CHAPTER 19

My Job

The Power of a Worthy Pursuit

From the time of Adam's fall, we have been required to earn a living. Adam was told, "By the sweat of your brow you will eat your food" (Genesis 3:19 NIV). In the New Testament, Paul is even more blunt: "The one who is unwilling to work shall not eat" (2 Thessalonians 3:10 NIV).

In passing, the Bible mentions some of the occupations of Bible characters. David was a shepherd, one of the humblest of jobs. Job and Abraham were herdsmen and became affluent. Peter, Andrew, James, and John were fishermen.

Jesus Himself grew up with His skilled tradesman father, Joseph, who was a carpenter. Paul was a tentmaker, as were his friends Priscilla and Aquila.

Because God ordains work and because He wants us to be happy, we should view work as an enjoyable pursuit. Most of the time I do enjoy my job, and on occasion, I've enjoyed my work so much that I've felt as if it were a pastime with pay.

But in any occupation, the time comes when we grow weary.

Perhaps the work is physically demanding or emotionally exhausting, or we may be under managers who make many unwise decisions. Or perhaps the problem is not with the work itself. The strain of an hour-long commute in heavy traffic can leave us exhausted before the workday even begins.

Do you often ask how you can remain enthusiastic at a thankless job in which you are unseen and unappreciated? If you are unable to find enjoyment in your job, then perhaps you can enjoy what the job allows you to do. Keep a pleasant disposition by thinking about how your salary will give your family an opportunity to do something pleasant together. The proper state of mind changes drudgery into a worthy pursuit. However, should you feel truly trapped in a dead-end job, preparing for a career change may be an option. But rather than taking an impulsive action, thoughtfully identify what you really want to accomplish, and work toward that goal.

Occasionally, we enjoy our work too much, or we chase after what money will bring to us. For many of us, the temptation to spend longer and longer hours at work can become a problem. Exodus 23:12 says, "Six days do your work, but on the seventh day do not work, so that your ox and your donkey may rest, and so that the slave born in your household and the foreigner living among you may be refreshed" (NIV).

A Christian worker should remember to take a break.

Unremitting labor will take a toll on the worker.

But it will also have a detrimental effect on the family of such a gung-ho personality. While the husband is working overtime, the wife must take on responsibilities beyond her own heavy load.

Children who have a part in sports events or school assemblies look in vain for the face of their father in the audience.

Their disappointment and the strain on the marriage can't be easily overcome by a larger paycheck.

⇀ Winning Respect ↽

*Make it your ambition to lead a quiet life:
You should mind your own business and work
with your hands, just as we told you, so that your daily
life may win the respect of outsiders and so that
you will not be dependent on anybody.*
1 Thessalonians 4:11–12 niv

⇀ Valuable Employee ↽

Lord, help me become a better worker. I will take the initiative to invest in myself by getting the training that will make me a more valuable employee. Help me anticipate change so I can prepare for it and be ready for the skills that new technology demands. Lord, the line between my work and my personal life is becoming more blurred every day. Guide me as I balance my work and my personal responsibilities.

⇥ Truth over Lies ⇤

Father, the custodian at work falsely signed that he had checked the fire extinguisher; the new applicant inflated his résumé; the manager counted rejected items as completed ones; the CEO released a quarterly report that won't bear close scrutiny. Lord, why has lying become so prevalent? Father, help me not to contribute to this culture. Give me no option but to choose truth over lies.

⇥ Moses' Prayer for Greater Leadership Skill ⇤

Moses said to the LORD, "You have been telling me, 'Lead these people,' but you have not let me know whom you will send with me. You have said, 'I know you by name and you have found favor with me.' If you are pleased with me, teach me your ways so I may know you and continue to find favor with you. Remember that this nation is your people."

EXODUS 33:12–13 NIV

⇥ Job Interview ⇤

Lord, it's time for me to seek advancement. At my job interview, help me make a good impression that correctly portrays what I can accomplish. I pray, Lord, that I will be offered a new job that is challenging and rewarding. But if the position isn't right for me, give me the patience to wait for You to present the right opportunity. Give Your blessing upon me as I seek a job that has Your endorsement.

⇀ Dressed for Success ↽

Lord, I've noticed people reading self-help books that give pointers on how to dress for success. Men are advised to dress conservatively in a dark two-piece business suit, button-down white shirt with tie, and dress shoes and matching belt. Lord, You have given us instructions for how to dress too. You tell us to put on Your armor—belt of truth, breastplate of righteousness, feet fitted with the Gospel, shield of faith, helmet of salvation, sword of the Spirit—to stand against the schemes of the devil.

⇀ Daily Chores ↽

Lord, my job can become a steady pounding of dreary, mundane tasks. They can seem to have no consequence or importance. Renew my passion for my daily responsibilities. I know You didn't create me to live a life of mediocrity but of excellence. Keep me from settling for second best. May Your presence be with me in the workplace. Let me be happy at my work and with what my work can bring to my family.

→ Jesus Completes His Work ←

"Father, the hour has come. Glorify your Son, that your Son may glorify you. For you granted him authority over all people that he might give eternal life to all those you have given him. Now this is eternal life: that they know you, the only true God, and Jesus Christ, whom you have sent. I have brought you glory on earth by finishing the work you gave me to do."
John 17:1–4 NIV

→ Serving the Public Good ←

Lord, I've read about Benjamin Franklin and how he used his printing shop to distribute songbooks and collections of prayers to the American colonies. The English authors of these books couldn't find a publisher in England because the authorities would not approve anything new. Franklin made a profit and at the same time served the public good. Lord, I pray my work will have a dual purpose of supporting my family and serving Christian objectives.

→ Public Persona ←

Lord, I understand that having a public persona that differs too widely from my private personality can cause stress. When I must bend my principles to meet the conditions of a job, stress is inevitable. Lord, free me from the need to be something I'm not. Lord,

I pray my Christian beliefs that are visible at home will shine through, unchanged, at work.

Overextended

Lord, I had a friend who overextended himself in an attempt to have it all. Then at a fund-raising dinner, he collapsed. Stress, the killer of men in their middle years, had almost taken its toll. Father, help me give balance to my life. May my drive at work never jeopardize my health, alienate my family, distance my friends, or detract from my service to You.

Swiftly Changing Circumstances

Lord, how can life move with such swift changes? One moment I have a good, steady job. Then suddenly my company merges with another. The reorganization leaves me with choices that will cause an upheaval in my family. Should I move, accept a lower-paying position, or find a job elsewhere? I'm left with doubt and indecision. Lord, I pray that no matter the turmoil around me, I will remain steadfast in knowing that You care about me.

Job Loss

Lord, the pink slips will go out tomorrow. Should I be one without a job, it will hurt. I pray You will be with me through the dark days. Help me avoid anger and frustration. Help me work through the practical problems of reworking my budget and maintaining health care. May I quickly move on to the next stage of my life. Lord, I have faith that You will open a new door for me.

⇁ Everything Comes from God ↽

"Wealth and honor come from you; you are the ruler of all things. In your hands are strength and power to exalt and give strength to all. Now, our God, we give you thanks, and praise your glorious name. But who am I, and who are my people, that we should be able to give as generously as this? Everything comes from you, and we have given you only what comes from your hand."
1 Chronicles 29:12–14 niv

⇁ My Company ↽

Lord, I pray for my place of employment. I want my company to be delighted with me as an employee, and I want to be pleased to be associated with my company. May the services we provide and products we sell be recognized as a positive contribution to our community. Guide my company to have a good reputation with both our suppliers and our customers. May the company prosper based on its creative efforts to offer products with real value.

⇸ My Supervisors ⇽

Lord, I pray for those in the workplace who manage and supervise. I know they must make difficult decisions. I pray they request and wisely evaluate input from all levels of the company. May they correctly balance their obligation to make a profit against the impact to workers and quality of products. I pray they will have a long-range vision to keep the company healthy as the economy changes.

CHAPTER 20

My Dreams

The Power to Surpass Myself

Waking dreams that go beyond daydreams call upon our better nature. We need dreams, goals, and aspirations. Without them, we would feed only our desire for pleasure. Forward-looking dreams create in us a stronger character by encouraging us to be more than we are now and opening a vista to a grander, richer tapestry of life. They cause us to aspire to excellence. Dreams are stirred up in a restless heart, one longing to be more, to do more, and to achieve more. Some dreams may be impulsive or fanciful. But others are more substantial. We can't shake them from our minds. They bubble to the top and survive even in the full light of day, challenging us to take them seriously.

God created us with the ability to dream. He leads us to think beyond our ordinary, moment-to-moment existence. When dreams take hold of us, we often look beyond what we want to do to what God wants to do through us. Suppressing these dreams means stifling a valuable experience that would give greater meaning to our lives. Should we reject them out of hand, we may ensure that we are all we are ever going to be.

Dreams require prayer. Before acting on them, we must seek the will of God. Difficult dreams are not those that require us to do something, but those that require us to change to succeed at them. For example, it couldn't have been easy for Peter to reject a lifetime of training to fulfill his vision from God to accept Gentiles as fellow Christians (Acts 10:34–35). And Paul, then known as Saul and an enemy of those who believed in Jesus, had to take the step of accepting Jesus as his Lord and Savior (Acts 9:17–19).

Dreams are fragile. By their very nature, they are private matters. In their early stages, they are incomprehensible to others. If we share dreams in their infancy, others may dismiss them, causing us to lose our vision. A patronizing review of our dreams can paralyze us into inaction. Criticism that our dreams can't be realized can cause us to lose confidence. Expose dreams to criticism only after they are fully protected by prayer and clothed in real-world practicality.

Dreams are dangerous, especially to the dreamer, as Joseph of the Old Testament found when his brothers sold him into slavery because of his dreams. His brothers are not the only ones who have said, "Let's kill the dreamer!" Fulfilling dreams requires courage. We may have our motives doubted, our intelligence disparaged, and our state of mind questioned. Or, worse, we may be simply ignored.

Dreams require commitment and endurance. "For the revelation awaits an appointed time; it speaks of the end and will not prove false. Though it linger, wait for it; it will certainly come and will not delay" (Habakkuk 2:3 NIV). The worth of a dream is exemplified by the difficulty of realizing it.

⇁ God's Marvelous Plans ↽

Lord, you are my God; I will exalt you and praise your name, for in perfect faithfulness you have done wonderful things, things planned long ago. . . . You have been a refuge for the poor, a refuge for the needy in their distress, a shelter from the storm and a shade from the heat. . . . In that day they will say, "Surely this is our God; we trusted in him, and he saved us. This is the Lord, we trusted in him; let us rejoice and be glad in his salvation."
Isaiah 25:1, 4, 9 NIV

⇁ When the Dreamer Wakes ↽

Lord, I'm intrigued by the question "When the dreamer wakes, what happens to the dream?" If I have a dream that You have put on my heart, but I put it aside after examining it in the cold light of day, what happens to that dream?

Is it lost forever, or do You impress it upon another person?

Father, help me discern the worthy goals You have given especially to me. May I keep them ever before me until they dawn to the full light of day.

⇾ Lost Dreams ⇽

Lord, many people plan on doing something special—someday. Then events occur that keep their dreams unfulfilled. One woman planned for the many tours she and her husband would take after they retired. But he died, and now she must travel alone. Lord, I too have dreams. Help me focus on worthy objectives, and provide me with the time to pursue them.

⇾ Chasing Grasshoppers ⇽

Lord, we have a dog that is obsessed with chasing grasshoppers. He never catches one, and I wonder what he would do if he did. Lord, I often seem to be chasing grasshoppers. No matter what I achieve, success stays out of reach. When I think clearly about what I want to achieve, I realize many of my ambitions aren't right for a Christian. I want to pursue what You would have me achieve rather than what I imagine would bring pleasure, success, and contentment.

⇾ Middle-Years Renewal ⇽

Lord, it wasn't until a few years ago that I began to realize that time is slipping rapidly through my fingers. If I ever want to do something special with my life, I have to begin now. Lord, help me see that the middle years are a time to grow. Give me confidence to use my skills and the resources You have provided to make a difference in the lives of those I meet.

⇾ Popularity ⇽

Lord, when I take my child to the playground, I notice that children tend to swarm around equipment based on its popularity with other children. A line forms at the slide while the climbing bars remain unused. The next time, the choice may be reversed. Lord, I sometimes find myself making decisions and setting goals based on what others are doing. I pray I will choose spiritual goals that honor You, regardless of popularity.

⇾ Kill the Dreamer ⇽

They saw [Joseph] in the distance, and before he reached them, they plotted to kill him. "Here comes that dreamer!" they said to each other. "Come now, let's kill him and throw him into one of these cisterns and say that a ferocious animal devoured him. Then we'll see what comes of his dreams"
GENESIS 37:18–20 NIV

⇢ Dreams, Goals, and Aspirations ⇠

Lord, dreams, goals, and aspirations are fine if I keep them to myself. But when I share them with others, critics immediately arise to put a damper on my enthusiasm. If I listen to them, they would convince me the best course of action is to do nothing. Lord, with Your guidance, I would rather strive for worthy goals and fall short than limit myself to easily obtainable goals of little significance.

⇢ Perfectly Plausible ⇠

Lord, when I awake in the morning and can remember dreams from the night before, I'm astonished at how incoherent some of them are. Yet in the dream everything seemed perfectly plausible. I wonder, however, if I'm much too logical and much too realistic in my waking hours. Often I have a goal or an aspiration that I dismiss as wildly improbable. Instead, Lord, help me strive to achieve those goals that have Your stamp of approval.

⇢ Realistic Goals ⇠

Lord, help me set realistic goals and not chase after vague, ill-conceived daydreams. Help me focus on attainments that make a difference and choose problems worthy of attack. Guide me in dividing the major objectives into smaller, readily achievable steps. I pray, Lord, that my goals will be in keeping with Your will and that my pursuit of them will strengthen my faith in Your guiding power.

⇾ Vital Goals ⇽

Lord, I've thought about the phenomenon known as the butterfly effect, in which a small, insignificant event has far-reaching consequences that can't be anticipated. What appear to be minor actions do have a way of reaching beyond the present and affecting eternity. Lord, help me set vital goals and recognize when a false step is leading me away from them. Help me steer clear of trivial details that may prevent me from reaching my goals.

⇾ Press On ⇽

Brothers and sisters, I do not consider myself yet to have taken hold of it. But one thing I do: Forgetting what is behind and straining toward what is ahead, I press on toward the goal to win the prize for which God has called me heavenward in Christ Jesus.
Philippians 3:13–14 niv

⇾ This Is the Moment ⇽

Lord, I've seen Christians who knew from an early age what their life's work should be. Their path toward it was straight as an arrow. Others, such as myself, are puzzled because we follow a long and winding way. But I have confidence an event will arise that perfectly matches my special abilities. Lord, when my calling is clearly visible, may I pursue it vigorously, never doubting Your purpose for me.

⇾ Later Than You Think ⇽

Lord, I took my father to an old home in the hills of Arkansas, where he'd lived as a child. We found an abandoned building with a sagging roof, vacant windows, and a yard overgrown with weeds. He saw in a sudden flash the passage of forty years. He said, "It's later than I thought." Time can take its toll on me too and give me a worn-out body, a dulled mind, or an overgrown soul. Lord, in my service to You, may I never utter the words "too late."

⇾ Middle-Aged ⇽

As middle age approaches, some of us panic. We think we are all we are ever going to be. We fear we will never realize unfulfilled dreams. Lord, I do have some unsatisfied goals. Even so, let me be happy regardless of my circumstances. Give me the contentment to know that wherever I am is where You want me to be.

⇁ Glittering Achievements ↽

Lord, I work with portable equipment with mind-blowing capability. Yet when the electrical circuit fails, the dead machine becomes an expensive door prop. You are the giver of dreams. When my aspirations aren't sanctioned by You, they become glittering achievements that are dead inside. Lord, keep me from basing my goals on my own desires. May I purge pride and selfishness when setting the direction of my life.

CHAPTER 21

My Fulfillment

The Power of Accepting God's Plan

In any person's life, the time comes when the question arises that demands an answer: Is this all there is? Even when a person has everything, the feeling persists that something's missing.

"I have a feeling this isn't life, is it?" Without an answer to the question, life has no peace and no purpose.

If a man consciously looks away to pretend the question doesn't exist, his life becomes hollow. Only by attending to the question, by accepting that God exists and that He has a plan for us, can we discover fulfillment.

Knowing Christ is the only path to true fulfillment. All other paths lead to emptiness. By accepting Christ, by living in the will of God, we find satisfaction. The Bible often tells of people who recognized that God had a purpose for them:

Paul (2 Timothy 3:10), David (Psalm 138:8), and others. The Bible says, " 'For I know the plans I have for you,' declares the Lord, 'plans to prosper you and not to harm you, plans to give you hope and a future'" (Jeremiah 29:11 NIV).

But when I became a Christian, the hollowness didn't entirely go away. I wanted to have a truly significant impact on my family and even the world. However, I thought I was wise enough to know what God intended for me. I pursued my own goals, but that led to emptiness. I recognized I needed to grow, but I focused on myself. The fulfillment was hollow. I needed not to concentrate on myself, but to center myself on God for Him to reveal His purpose for me. Pursuing God's goals leads to fulfillment.

God wants my heart more than any works I might do.

To find fulfillment, I first must grow a satisfying relationship with God. Then I can see the difference between serving myself and serving God. When I'm no longer preoccupied with my own fulfillment, I can see more clearly those opportunities that God provides. My fulfillment comes from reaching goals put before me by Jesus rather than goals I set for myself.

Are you seeking fulfillment? Then immediately begin doing what you can with what you have rather than wishing for more. You need not be overly concerned about your current limitations. God said to Israel, "So do not fear, for I am with you; do not be dismayed, for I am your God. I will strengthen you and help you; I will uphold you with my righteous right hand" (Isaiah 41:10 NIV).

God offers many opportunities to do good: defending the cause of the weak and fatherless and maintaining the rights of the poor and oppressed (Psalm 82:3), binding up the brokenhearted (Isaiah 61:1), visiting the sick and captive (Matthew 25:39), and bringing salvation to the lost (Matthew 28:19). The grace of Jesus, the love of God, and the guidance of the Holy Spirit will direct you to a special cause that will bring true fulfillment.

⇁ Prayer for Fulfillment ↽

Have mercy on me, my God, have mercy on me, for in you I take refuge. I will take refuge in the shadow of your wings until the disaster has passed. I cry out to God Most High, to God, who vindicates me. He sends from heaven and saves me, rebuking those who hotly pursue me—God sends forth his love and his faithfulness.
Psalm 57:1–3 niv

⇁ Mission for the Lord ↽

Lord, I know You have a work for me. You shine Your light on me and illuminate the path that will lead to my destiny. When I understand my special mission, I pray I will accept it and not stop short. May I seize it with wholehearted determination. Lord, with Your strength, I will follow through to its successful completion. I offer thanksgiving and praise that I can be of service to You.

⇾ Emptiness ⇽

Lord, when I go into an empty room, I turn on the lights. If I must wait in the room for a while, I will pick up something to read or turn on music or the television. I can't long endure darkness or silence. Lord, when I have emptiness in my life, I rush to fill the void. I will come to You in prayer to fill my life with joy, love, kindness, and the other fruits of the Spirit.

⇾ Volunteering ⇽

Lord, You gave Paul the opportunity to mention one of the statements of Jesus that isn't found anywhere in the Gospels: "It is more blessed to give than to receive" (Acts 20:35 NIV). When I spend some time in volunteer work, I always end the session feeling better than when I began. Occasionally, I can do the volunteer effort with my family. We are brought closer together through the shared experience. Thank You for giving me the opportunity to serve others and bring fulfillment to our family.

⇾ Solomon's Prayer for Wisdom ⇽

Solomon answered, "You have shown great kindness to your servant, my father David, because he was faithful to you and righteous and upright in heart. You have continued this great kindness to him and

*have given him a son to sit on his throne this very day. . . .
So give your servant a discerning heart to govern your
people and to distinguish between right and wrong.
For who is able to govern this great people of yours?"*
1 KINGS 3:6, 9 NIV

⇾ RENEWAL ⇽

Lord Jesus, I'm often in need of renewal. Anxiety, discouragement, and physical and spiritual exhaustion take their toll. I know You prayed for others, but You also prayed for Yourself. I now come before You and humbly ask You to attend to my special needs. Lord, these personal requests benefit only me.

Provided they are in Your will, I ask that they be granted.

⇾ CAPACITY ⇽

Lord, I showed my son a glass filled to the midpoint with water. I asked him what he saw, thinking he would give either the pessimistic answer of half empty or the optimistic answer of half full. Instead, he said the glass was too big for its contents. Lord, I realize my expectations can exceed my capacity. I pray I will understand that fulfillment comes from doing what I can with what I have rather than wishing for more.

→ Motivation ←

Lord, as my school and college career progressed, I discovered that someone always rose to be better than me in any particular subject. Lord, I'm thankful You don't measure me by the abilities of others. You use me whether I'm at the top of the class or struggling to pass. But I must strive to rise to the ability You have given me. Thank You for measuring my value by my willingness to serve You.

→ Throne of Honor ←

Then Hannah prayed and said: "My heart rejoices in the Lord; in the Lord my horn is lifted high. My mouth boasts over my enemies, for I delight in your deliverance. . . . The Lord sends poverty and wealth; he humbles and he exalts. He raises the poor from the dust and lifts the needy from the ash heap; he seats them with princes and has them inherit a throne of honor. For the foundations of the earth are the Lord's; on them he has set the world."
1 Samuel 2:1, 7–8 niv

→ Latent Energy ←

Lord, when I studied physics, I learned about latent energy—hidden energy that could be brought out under the right circumstances. As Your special creation, I have the capacity for growth and development. Let me not be concerned about my current limitations. Instead, help me work toward my hidden promise. I ask You to bring out my full potential. I want to be a tool in Your hands to achieve what I'm capable of doing.

⇁ Person of Distinction ↽

Lord, I know character can't be constructed in a moment. It must be built over a lifetime of making the right choices and taking the correct actions. Help me build my character with the building blocks of honesty, honor, helpfulness, and humility. I pray I will always be mindful of what builds my character and avoid those actions that tarnish it. May I succeed while maintaining my integrity.

⇁ Seeing the Future ↽

Lord, I earnestly seek a faith determined to please You. You have guided me this far, and I pray I will accept Your plan for my life until I have fulfilled my destiny. I ask that You open my eyes to Your Word as specific guidance for me in particular. I have received daily blessings from You, and I desire to continue in the way that leads to the final blessing of being with You forever.

⇾ Glorious Name ⇽

And the Levites. . .said: "Stand up and praise the Lord your God, who is from everlasting to everlasting. Blessed be your glorious name, and may it be exalted above all blessing and praise. You alone are the Lord. You made the heavens, even the highest heavens, and all their starry host, the earth and all that is on it, the seas and all that is in them. You give life to everything, and the multitudes of heaven worship you."
Nehemiah 9:5–6 niv

⇾ Best Years ⇽

Lord, on the street where my parents live, couples whose children are grown occupy most homes. Some of my parents' neighbors live in tight financial conditions. A few have medical conditions that limit their activities. Others are of retirement age but must work part-time jobs. Yet I see that those who have embraced You view these years as the best times of their lives. I'm learning that Your peace is far more wonderful than I can understand.

⇾ Top Off ⇽

Lord, before my family and I leave on a long driving trip, I check the car. In addition to topping off all of the fluid levels, I replenish a small survival kit and check the air pressure in the spare. Lord, my life is a long journey. I need to replenish myself for the journey through prayer and meditation on Your Word. I ask that I complete the journey successfully and be welcomed into heaven, my final destination.

⇾ Mold Me ⇽

Lord, I'm fascinated with unfinished or incomplete works of art: Venus de Milo's missing arms, Gilbert Stuart's unfinished portrait of George Washington, and Beethoven's unfinished Tenth Symphony. Whether by accident, death, or intention, they represent the tension of a work left in limbo. Lord, I know I'm a work in progress, but I ask You to continue to shape me. I know You won't abandon me, and I'm willing to be clay that is molded in Your hands.

Conclusion

It is my hope that you have been blessed as you considered these passages of scripture and the prayers accompanying them. I pray that you have discovered or been reminded of the many ways you have been blessed by our wonderful heavenly Father.

Throughout the year, as you encounter both good experiences and bad, stop and remember that God intends to bless you. As a good Father, He only means to bring things into your life that will contribute to your good and His glory.

I have always teased my Southern friends that they can say or do absolutely anything so long as they follow it up with "Bless your heart." In fact, I've often heard one of my Southern friends say something otherwise offensive but smooth it over with that phrase. "She can't fix her hair to save her life, bless her heart."

In some ways, the fact that God only wishes to bless us should make the dictates of His will more palatable. That missing promotion, that long line of traffic, that undeserved criticism are for our good.

So live for Him. Take graciously from His hand whatever He gives.

Bless your heart!

If you, then, though you are evil, know how to give good gifts to your children, how much more will your Father in heaven give good gifts to those who ask him!
MATTHEW 7:11 NIV